'Writing with incredible ⸻
Mukwashi deconstruc⸻ ⸻⸻
of identity. A celebration of diversity and belonging, her
fascinating story argues for a world that's enhanced by our
differences but grounded in our shared humanity.'
Rt. Hon. David Lammy MP

'Amanda Khozi Mukwashi tells her personal history, woven
into a story of humanity. It is vivid, dignified, wistful and
defiant. It demands a change in how we regard each other and
whom we value. Deeply impressive.'
Sarah Sands, Editor of the BBC *Today* programme

'*But where are you really from?*' is a timely, insightful, and
important book. In answering that seemingly simple but
meaning laden question Amanda Khozi Mukwashi offers a
deeply personal account that illuminates a universal truth:
Each of us, wherever we come from, has a story worth hearing
and each of us are worthy of dignity and love. In these troubled
times this book reminds us that our differences shouldn't be a
source of fear ... they are a source of interest and respect.'
Douglas Alexander, former International Development
Secretary of State

'This book is a wonderful example of the power of storytelling.
But where are you really from? weaves together a rich tapestry
of journeys that took place long before her birth, the personal
paths Amanda has taken and how she has been shaped by
them. By vulnerably sharing the lessons she has learned about
herself and the world from this rich tapestry of stories, the

book speaks with a clear and urgent voice about the path we need to take to recognise each other as fully human. This is a story we need to keep hearing over and over again, until the much-needed change we seek in seeking dignity, equality and justice for all people – no matter where they are from - is achieved.'

Chine McDonald, writer, broadcaster and regular presenter of BBC Radio 4's *Thought for the Day*

'I remember the first time I met Amanda Khozi Mukwashi at Westminster Abbey on the 4th April 2018 at the Christian Aid service in honour of the late great Dr Martin Luther King Jr organised by my brother Richard Reddie. The service was to mark the life and legacy of Dr Martin Luther King Jr. I believe it was also Amanda's second day in her new role as the Chief Executive of Christian Aid. I remember the impromptu speech she gave in the following symposium at the nearby St Margaret's Church, that was stunning in its insight and imagination. This book is an opportunity to hear the back story to one of the most important Black Christian woman presently living and working in the UK. Amanda Khozi Mukwashi is a trailblazer and an inspiration to many and this book explains why! It is a must read.'

Professor Anthony Reddie, Director of the Oxford Centre for Religion and Culture at Regent's Park College, Oxford University. He is also an Extraordinary Professor with the University of South Africa. He was awarded the Archbishop of Canterbury's 2020 Lanfranc award for services to Education and Scholarship.

'What a great read! Amanda Khozi Mukwashi is the lioness who tells a hopeful story of how we have far more in common if only we reach beyond lazy assumptions about colour or gender or origin. Amanda could easily be 'from' Coventry, Malawi, Rome, Twickenham, Zambia, or Zimbabwe but that doesn't matter so much if, wherever you go, the trees know your name. Hers is a story grounded in heritage, faith and purpose, and one that should inspire all of us to explore our own stories and challenge the assumptions we make about others' stories.'

Danny Sriskandarajah, CEO, Oxfam GB

'Amanda Khozi Mukwashi shares with her readers a life reflecting family ambition and expectation; of the dreams of her ancestors combined with the dedication of her immediate family who modelled courage, resilience and agency. 'The trees knows her name, and the very earth, also knows her name' – now we and a generation to come will also know her name and by educating ourselves, knowing where we are coming from and ready to navigate where we are going – we will embrace the trees that will know our names too.

Amanda, carrying the hopes and the dreams of those gone before her, enables her readers to see black people with new lens – having navigated two major obstacles: cultural limitations due to one's gender and a majority ethnic population here in Europe always attempting to limit one's ability due to skin colour. This book will be a real gift to those who take the time to stop and read it.'

The Rt Rev Rose Hudson-Wilkin CD, MBE, Bishop of Dover

'Ms Amanda Khozi Mukwashi's *But where are you really from?* is a gripping, tear-jerking, humbling yet empowering story of stories that, once you've picked it up, it's very difficult to want to put (it) down. The title of this story of stories publication evokes and provokes all sorts of vexed and vexing questions, feelings and emotions in most of us who have been colonised or disadvantaged or oppressed in one way or another, stripped of y/our identity, heritage and dignity. What may come across as a "simple" question of your origin becomes heavily loaded this and that way, laying bare what lurks deepest underneath a myriad layers of skin colour, class, gender and more that tend to define who you are and how others choose to define you. In a most penetrating and incisive manner, Amanda has brought us a lot closer to understanding ramifications that come with who we or you are. A political economy master class penned passionately and expressed eloquently between these covers of *But where are you really from?* I wish *I* was the author, as it is to me, of me and about me and, yes, us, any- and everywhere...'
Morakabe Raks Seakhoa, poet, activist, former Robben Island prisoner, MD of the wRite associates and Director of the South African Literary Awards and Africa Century International African Writers Conference and founder CEO of the Maritime Heritage Institute

BUT WHERE ARE YOU REALLY FROM?

On identity, humanhood and hope

Amanda Khozi Mukwashi

First published in Great Britain in 2020

Society for Promoting Christian Knowledge
36 Causton Street
London SW1P 4ST
www.spck.org.uk

British Library Cataloguing-in-Publication Data
A catalogue record for this book is available from the British Library

ISBN 978 0 281 08541 5
eBook ISBN 978 0 281 08542 2

1 3 5 7 9 10 8 6 4 2

Typeset by The Book Guild Ltd, Leicester, UK
Printed and bound by CPI Group (UK) Ltd, Croydon, CR0 4YY

eBook by The Book Guild Ltd, Leicester, UK

Produced on paper from sustainable forests

For

My mother: she is clothed in love, strength and dignity
Mbuya na Sekuru: they ran a good race

Contents

Foreword

ROWAN WILLIAMS

I won't be the only reader to be brought up short by Amanda's story of her grandfather telling her that the trees know her name – that there is a place where she is simply recognized as who and what she is, at home with a creation she is fully part of.

One way of thinking about the monumental and pervasive sin that is racial injustice is to see it as a denial of this kind of at-homeness to the greater part of humanity. Those who dominate the global economy and the workings of a self-styled 'developed' world have created an environment in which those without economic leverage are denied not just the liberty to co-operate in shaping and humanising the world around, but the deeper liberty to experience the world as their world, their habitat, their home. They are recognized only to the extent that they collaborate in a project that someone else defines for them. The map is drawn with all the lines converging on the powerful; everyone's place is fixed with reference to the 'centres' where financial decisions are made. The further you stand from those centres, the more likely it is that in one way or another you will be asked to prove that you have a right to be attended to. The more likely it is that – literally or metaphorically – you will be asked to show your papers. And part of what we in the wealthy world and the wealthy sectors of local societies are being asked to see is that these 'centres' are not just the offices of international finance, but the minds and hearts of all of us who take for granted the workings of this system in our own patterns of expectation and consumption – who in practice accept the 'normality' of power relations that have historically entrenched white privilege and white exceptionalism. We may say truthfully enough that we are not guilty of prejudice, that we have no desire to reinforce the oppression of the world's non-white majority; but we inherit and profit from the mechanisms that created these sinful structures.

When we are told this, the reaction is often to push away the pain of acknowledging that we stand in this line of inheritance. Yet it is a mistake to think of this in a forensic way, as if we white readers had to plead either guilty or not guilty. The issue is not about individual guilt in the first instance but about seeing more clearly, learning new kinds of recognition, understanding the scope of what has been done to deprive others of their world. The question then is not about how I lament my guilt, but about how I join in the labour needed to recognize and restore; how I take responsibility for moving the world closer to a pattern of genuinely shared space and stability, well-being and mutual life-giving.

What Amanda does here is to issue this summons to action by telling her own story of learning and witness, a story in which what she learns from her local and family identity becomes part of what she offers to a global project of creating equity and lasting mutuality. She does not pretend this is a simple task; she does not romanticize a lost past or suggest that a few cosmetic reforms will do the trick. And the burden of that hard honesty is made bearable for her by the knowledge that there is a life-giving truth to which all are answerable: the abundant, limitless love in which we are created has given us a world in which each is called to find a place of dignity and creative authority. If the trees know our names, it is because their maker and ours eternally speaks the name of each and every being that is created, and holds it in unchanging, faithful affirmation. The task of human faith is to grow in confident awareness of this eternal affirmation and to speak it out and act it out whoever and wherever we are – learning to know each other's names in the fullest possible way.

This is a book that tells the story of a woman of depth, strength, courage and integrity – a woman I have had the privilege of working with and learning from in Christian Aid. We are blessed in having someone like this in leadership at Christian Aid. This book allows a wider public to share that blessing, and I welcome it with great gratitude.

Acknowledgements

There is nothing without God.

My mother has been the central pillar of my upbringing. She provided me with life lessons, a sense of belonging and unconditional love. The richness of the stories that have contributed to me being me come in large part from her and her parents. When I first told her that I wanted to write this book, she was excited and very encouraging. That enthusiasm has continued throughout. She has filled in the gaps that I had; she has explained some of the context that I did not fully understand as a child. She has been my greatest supporter. As always. I am thankful to God for my mother, she is an extraordinary human being. It is because of her that I had a wonderful relationship with my maternal grandparents.

My grandparents, Vute and Grace, lived a life of goodness. They provided a great foundation for many people to flourish. They left a legacy beyond the material. The village they built, while no longer physically there, is something that I carry within me. This book would not have been possible without them. May their souls continue to rest in peace.

I want to thank my sister Mercy for walking this journey with me. For the lengthy conversations about our shared history, for remembering and helping me to remember. For shared laughter. For always praying for me and seeing good in me. Thank you

There are a number of people who have been so supportive

and have shown extraordinary willingness and commitment for me to succeed in writing and completing this book. A huge thank you to Mbozi Haimbe for being an inspiration to me. She helped me to have the courage to switch on my laptop and start typing. Just write, she said, and I did. Together with Afua Twum-Danso Imoh, Chine McDonald and Dionne Gravesande, they took time to read my mutterings and gave me amazing feedback. They had discussions with me, asked me questions, helped me clarify my thoughts. They heard me. Thank you

A special mention for James Macintyre. For your support, encouraging words and affirming me as I speak out on issues of social justice. Thank you.

There are several friends who, like me, have a heritage that cuts across two or more countries. I spoke to them while doing some of my research, to hear their experiences. I am grateful that they shared their stories with me. I hope they too find the voice and space to tell their own stories in their own ways. It was to my friends that I ran to ensure that my spellings in Shona were fine. I am grateful to Busi Mhlanga and Musi Katerere for checking my Shona (Karanga spellings)! Thank you.

As a novice in writing, I had no clue how to get onto the publishing ladder or what it would entail. Chine was selfless in introducing me to Elizabeth Neep, who energized me and guided me through the process! Elizabeth has been an amazing publisher and I want to thank her and her team for working so hard and so quickly to have this book published. For keeping the integrity of my story and the authenticity of my voice. Thank you.

Acknowledgements

I have learnt a lot from my time at Christian Aid. The deep caring that people bring to their jobs, for each other and for the mission of the organization. The commitment and desire to see transformation happen. The belief that good can come out if only we stay committed. The willingness to have difficult conversations and find ways to heal. A fabulous Board with an incredible Chair in Rowan Williams, who has created the space for different voices to be heard. Thank you for being part of my story of stories.

My stories started in the home and it is in the home that they have flourished. A loving environment that is nurturing and affirming has been my bedrock. It was in my home that I talked endlessly about the stories. My husband, daughter and son – three wonderful individuals who keep me grounded – listened and listened and listened some more. Sometimes they got bored, I think at times they were irritated (especially during the lockdown), but still they listened, commented, laughed with me and encouraged me. Thank you, Lord, for blessing me with a wonderful family.

> 'The earth is the Lord's, and everything in it. The world and all its people belong to him.'
>
> Psalm 24:1

UNTIL THE LIONESS
LEARNS TO TELL
HER STORY,
THE STORY OF
HUNTING WILL
ALWAYS GLORIFY
THE HUNTER –
TRADITIONAL
AFRICAN PROVERB.

1

But where are you really from?

'Where are you from?' I'm asked.
'The UK,' I reply.
'I mean where are you really from?'
'Zambia,' I reply.

Where are you from? It's a common question. A question that helps to open conversations, allows us to connect through shared stories and brings us closer together as we affirm each other, our common heritage and our humanhood. It establishes our kinship. In most cases, this question is for those who look like us, sound like us and come from the same nation, region or town. It's a kinship. For many people from visible ethnic minorities in the UK, however, this question is almost always followed by another question: But where are you really from? A simple question. One that is very familiar to those who have had to answer this question many times in their lives. As a Black woman born and currently living in the UK, I have lost count of the number of times that I have been asked it. And, simple though the question may seem, the issues that simmer beneath it are infinitely more complicated.

Let's assume for a moment that it is you who has asked *me* the question. Already a complexity of emotions is bubbling up inside of me. At times, I find myself pre-empting the question

1

completely and introducing myself as being 'originally' from Zambia – perhaps a defence mechanism? Other times I find it mildly irritating, very frustrating and even insulting. Then there are the times where I am just plain disappointed, where I feel let down because I think you should know better. While it may not have been your intention – and while I cannot speak for all visible ethnic minority groups – for me, this simple question is loaded with a subtle, sometimes even subconscious, intention: to place me on a weighing scale. You may say, 'but where are *you* really from?' but instead I hear, 'where are you in relation to me.'

It is a question that means different things depending upon the ethnicity, colour of skin and perhaps accent of the person being asked. For some, the question might be posed to ascertain whether you are from a community or country that is perceived as being dangerous and therefore whether you could be a dangerous person – the message being, 'I don't trust you'. For others, the question might mean, 'I think you are uneducated, primitive, suffering and desperate' – the message being, 'I pity you'. However it is asked, the question of where are you really from dismisses any response to the initial question (Where are you from?), rejects your offer of a shared humanity and goes in search of what makes us 'other', different and what grounds there are for exclusion. The question is a loaded one and the answer will define and shape the parameters of your initial engagement with me.

In my opinion, starting a conversation with the question 'Where are you really from?' is not about origin. I could say I am from anywhere, a place you might not even have heard of and that would not matter to you at all. What you want to

2

know is what values and beliefs do I have? What has shaped me and how will I behave? All fair questions to ask when you want to get to know someone. The challenge is that you already have an answer. Whether you like me in colour or gender, you have looked at me and, more often than not, you have reached some initial conclusions. Now that would not be so bad, except that you have based your initial conclusion on the colour of my skin and the fact that I am a woman. By just looking at the fact that my skin colour is different from yours and acting on your instincts to ask me where I am from, you have stripped me of any connection to you, the assumption being: I am other.

With this question come the assumptions, images and narratives that you know of or have seen on television, social media or that are based upon what you have been told by those whom you trust. Assumptions that have shaped your views of and conclusions about people who are visibly different from you. Whatever my answer to the question is, it is a trigger in your mind that sets a whole series of thoughts in process, including where you think you stand in relation to me (only it is not in relation to me as an individual, but is in relation to my colour and everything you think it stands for). Silently – again, sometimes subconsciously – you weigh my intelligence, my physical attributes, my abilities, my motives, my values and ideals and, ultimately, my humanhood. You conclude that I weigh slightly less than other racial, gender and continental groups. So with that weighing comes a lowering of the rights that are due to me, giving you permission to treat me as a second-class citizen. It says I am not in the same league as you. It frees your mind from having to acknowledge that we are both human beings.

3

To some, this complex reaction to a seemingly simple question may seem extreme, but I believe we find ourselves yet again in a time where we need to say enough is enough to any kind of racism, regardless of whether due to ill intent, ignorance or naivety. Simple questions and single narratives are the very thing that change the minds of people and rob others of their humanhood. To the point where a government can systematically target hard working and law-abiding individuals who have lived in the UK all their lives, removing them from their only known home to deport them to a place of 'origin'. Or where a handful of policemen think it is alright to casually squeeze the life out of an unarmed Black man on the streets of Minneapolis. For you, maybe it is the 'Black woman' that has been painted in a negative light: articulation is heard as loud, assertiveness is seen as aggression, our physical features are too much of everything – too big, too wide, too thin, just too much. For me, on my best days, the 'Black woman' represents power, one that has been forced down into the ground but needs to erupt like a volcano, bursting forth with the strength and passion that is needed for change. Yes, single narratives are simple – but they are not who we are. Until we share and own our multifaceted stories, these ostracizing 'simple' questions will persist.

As someone who comes from a culture of oral storytelling, I am convinced that, 'until the lioness learns to tell her story, the story of hunting will always glorify the hunter'. For too long, stories have been told by the few and the world has been shaped around their untruths, half-truths and single perspectives. The next phase of this journey must be based on different stories and new truths. I want to tell you a story, or, more accurately, a set of stories about how a strong heritage can easily be lost or can be transformational as one searches to conform to or inform the dominant narrative in the context in which it lives. I also want to pass this multicultural heritage of mine to the next generation, especially in a world where each piece of the heritage appears to only come with baggage and prejudice.

What many in the next generation know of the different pieces of my heritage is based on an experience that is skewed through the lens of a distorted story of what is good, beautiful and acceptable – one that has been scripted by others who are only able to define themselves by making everything else that is not theirs ugly. This denial of beauty, intelligence and wisdom is a denial of the existence of other equal human beings. It is a denial of a difference that is equally valuable and significant. For the next generation, it is a denial of what makes them them. I hope that, in telling this story of stories, not only will it help me to reclaim my lost heritage, but that it will also help those who read it to discover and enjoy what we thought was lost and what they can be. We need to tell our stories of hope and defiance to overcome the untruths that seek to still a heritage of good things. I am not naive, but I am hopeful. My hope is built on the strong foundations of pieces that I have picked up on my journey. I want to tell this story – a continuous journey of learning and growing.

So where am I really from? A simple question with a multifaceted answer. As a Black woman born and living in the UK, I have been influenced by some of the values and ideals of the people who live here, whether indigenous to the UK or migrants from the rest of Europe, Africa, Asia, Latin

America or the Caribbean. In a melting pot of many different cultures, one cannot fail to pick up some universal value pieces beyond race and gender from others, and vice versa, as we continuously develop and evolve as human beings to become the best versions of ourselves and our human race. You'll see from my story that we have more in common than we can appreciate in one lifetime. Maybe instead of asking, 'But where are you really from?', you could ask me who I am instead?

I AM THE DAUGHTER OF A SHONA WOMAN AND A NGONI MAN.

I am the product of two great nations. I accept that I am different. I walk confidently, knowing that I am a product of strength, of love and of humanness.

2

Origins and identity

'I'm *originally* from Zambia...' I've already told you I sometimes choose to pre-empt the question of my origin. You see the stories of my life, of any life, cannot be confined to a short and simple response. If we were speaking of our *true* origin, that would be different; mine – like yours – began as an idea in another's mind before taking shape as a micro something in the womb; each of us equal and with innate worth. The story of identity, however, has a much longer trajectory for me, one that continues to evolve even now.

My identity, like yours, is one that has been shaped and continues to be reshaped by different experiences and beliefs. Over the years, I have been on a journey. So too were my parents before me and their parents before them. During these journeys, values and practices have evolved, been enhanced or re-affirmed and dreams reshaped as the different generations have interacted with others and learned new things. I know that, for as long as this journey is ongoing, so will the process of learning, unlearning and relearning, as I pick up new and different stories. Different parts that come from many different 'peoples', communities, societies and beliefs, including those that you consider your own.

These pieces have brought me to this point in time in this place – the UK – that I now fondly call my second home, albeit a home fraught with historical wrongs and distortions, one that struggles with its current realities of race and power, but a home nevertheless, that provides sanctuary to many. Yet to understand how I got here, you have to understand where I have been. For now, let me start my stories from a couple of generations back in another place I call home.

Africa. What images does that name conjure for you? A thousand stereotypes persist. Africa is not one ethnic group, not a community, not a country – it is a continent. In fact, it is such a big continent made up of so many countries, hosting so much diversity and so many histories within it, that most of what is written does not do it justice. The 54[1] countries in Africa represent so many different social groups who speak different languages, practice thousands of cultural norms and have been on the move for generations. A few of the groups are divided by natural borders such as rivers, while the majority were divided by the 1854–55 Berlin Conference, where 'Europe's arbitrary post-colonial borders left Africans bunched into countries that don't represent their heritage, a contradiction that still troubles them today.'[2]

During that period, Africa then, as it is now, was the battle ground for European powers who were fighting for economic, social and political dominance. Much European interaction with Africa over the centuries has primarily been about economics; the economics of exploitation of resources and of people. In the process of creating this dominance, a key aspect during the colonial era was to remove all sense of pride, beliefs and identity and replace them with a European view of the

---

1   As at August 2020.

2   <https://www.theatlantic.com/international/archive/2012/09/
    the-dividing-of-a-continent-africas-separatist-problem/262171/>

world, of religion and of values and practices. Having managed to strip the African slaves, taken hundreds of years before, of their identity, this can be seen as the second part of the siege on all things African. This exploitation continues to this day, albeit in a different form of capitalism.

Southern Africa was largely colonized by the British, with the Dutch, the Portuguese and the Germans scrambling for some other parts. I like to describe it as lions fighting over a chunk of meat. The reality, however, is that there was nothing majestic or great about the brutal bloodshed, oppression and enslavement of entire nations. So I would rather describe it more like hyenas, opportunistic, devious and ruthless, the stronger among the pack ending up with the greater chunks. In the case of Africa and, indeed, Southern Africa, it was like being torn apart by scavengers while alive. The people of Southern Africa were always on the move, trying to find relief from the brutality of the colonizers while retaining some of their beliefs, values and identities.[3]

Deep in the heart of Southern Africa, you will find the Shona: a proud and strong people, with a rich history – the builders of 'the Great Zimbabwe, extensive stone ruins of an African Iron Age city.'[4] The place itself lies in southeastern Zimbabwe, about 19 miles southeast of Masvingo, formerly known as Fort Victoria.

---

3 The story of Kunta Kinte (although not from Southern Africa) aka. 'the slave who fought back' well captures the spirit of those who were always on the move. His journey starts in 1767 when he was captured in the surrounding forests of his home village at the age of 17, sold into slavery and taken to America. Kunta Kinte became the inspiration for, and lead character in one of the world's bestselling novels, *Roots: The Saga of an American Family*, written by African-American author Alex Haley.

4 <https://www.britannica.com/place/Great-Zimbabwe>

From among the Shona, a young man and woman emerge. They get married, start a family and together they set off to find the proverbial greener pastures, crossing the Zambezi river from the then Southern Rhodesia to Northern Rhodesia (both former British colonies, now known as Zimbabwe and Zambia, respectively). Across rivers and their lifetimes, they nurture their values, their beliefs and their identities, passing them onto their children and grandchildren in the hope that the essence of who they are and what they stand for will live on and not die. One of those grandchildren is me.

In my search to reclaim and celebrate the pieces of my heritage that have been lost, I cannot understate the importance of capturing and understanding the journey taken by my grandfather, Vute – known as *Sekuru* to me – and my grandmother, Grace – known as *Mbuya*. Some of my knowledge naturally comes from my own experience with Sekuru and Mbuya, some of it comes from my mother and some comes from the remaining living members of this community from their generation. My grandmother herself passed on in 2016 at an estimated 92 years of age – although it was said that she was a few years older than that. I am worried that with the passing of time, all knowledge of the different stories will be lost, and so I must make haste and listen to the one or two remaining peers who remember their journey, one that represents the thousands of people and voices who made the peaceful journey in search of a new home. I need to put the pieces together and I am living in the building as I build it.

I start my story of identity with my maternal grandparents Sekuru and Mbuya because, despite being brought up in a highly patriarchal society, they nevertheless took centre stage in my life and the lives of my siblings. They championed a different approach to life, particularly with regard to the role of 'the girl'; they were pioneers of change in the small places where it mattered most – the home, where the essence of who I am today was cultivated and nurtured. At times they were hard, as would be expected of those who played their part in the liberation struggle for their people, but they always upheld principles of integrity and respect, truth, honesty and love, at times even to their detriment.

As they travelled, Sekuru and Mbuya were also accompanied by Sekuru's mother, my great grandmother, and their 'hama' (relatives or extended family). One notable senior cousin who travelled with cattle is called *Bhudi*. Bhudi (a prefix used to refer to an older brother as a sign of respect) Bhudi is now in his eighties and lives in the central province of Zambia. A permanent fixture during my childhood, he was always there or being referred to as the 'go-to' person for answers. In a way similar to how my grandparents challenged notions of what a 'girl's' role was, Bhudi was also an anomaly among my mother's people. Where they generally spoke loudly and firmly, he was very gentle and softly spoken. Despite Bhudi being a close member of the family, he was not someone I could claim to have known very well, along with several other members of the extended family; I guess I was just a kid, so to me, Bhudi seemed far too old to have any regular direct interaction with. However, as a I look back and reflect, he stands out as the embodiment of family, hard work and love, three elements that were ever present and central to the journey that Sekuru and Mbuya embarked upon and the life they built around themselves. As one of the oldest members of the family remaining, Bhudi is now one of perhaps two or three people in that age group in our family who I know of that remember the journey, albeit quite blurrily. He was just a young boy when he journeyed with my grandparents as they passed a small town named Hwange - then Wankie – to cross the Zambezi river that ran through Livingstone town.

The town of Livingstone is home to the Victoria Falls – the Mosi-oa-Tunya (the smoke that thunders) – so named by the locals because of the vapour that comes up as the water falls and hits the rocks beneath. From afar, you can see the vapour as it rises in the sky like smoke, and you can hear the water as it drops like thunder. The explorer David Livingstone renamed the falls after Great Britain's Queen Victoria, and the town was named after him. Although I have no issue with patriots wanting to name great things after their own people, I do take issue with the missed opportunity to tell the story of the local people.

Each time the name Mosi-oa-Tunya is mentioned, there are many stories that one could tell of the people, the knowledge and the culture of this beautiful place. The re-naming of this town and falls in the colonial era means that each time the origin of its name is asked, the story told is one of a conquered people and the honouring of a woman who had nothing to do with its glory, nor appreciated it. Sadly, the importance of naming has been lost and, in a seemingly meaningless way, a piece of the heritage and narrative of the people of Livingstone, the *Toka-leya*, has been stolen with it.

Sekuru and his family passed Mosi-oa-Tunya as they made the crossing sometime between 1945 and 1957. This period saw a huge number of people from among the Shona and Ndebele ethnic groups of Southern Rhodesia migrate to Northern Rhodesia on the invitation of the then Governor, Sir Roland 'Roy' Welensky. In history books and other new media, Welensky is described as a politician and, at some point, he was Prime Minister of the Federation of Rhodesia and Nyasaland.[5] Truth be told, he was just another greedy capitalist who believed that Black people were less human than White. He represented a racist and White supremacist era that exploited both the people and resources of what is now Zambia, Zimbabwe and Malawi, as well as many other countries on the African continent.

A lot has already been written of the exploits of those who colonized Africa. Those accounts represent a particular view and experience based on what the colonizers thought they saw and understood, and what justified their actions. In telling my story of stories, it is important to look through the eyes of those who experienced this oppression, this trampling of identities and robbing of dignity, humanhood and land. This is what Sekuru and Mbuya lived through.

When I look at the world as it is in the 21st century, with a global economy that is broken and unable to meet the needs of the poorest in our communities, a definition of prosperity that is short-sighted and based on feeding an unquenchable hunger and an exploitation of resources that has placed both people and planet in danger of destruction, I see that not much has changed since the time of my grandparents' crossing. I still see how those who are living in extreme poverty are perpetually trying to catch up. I recognize that the power structures and

---

5   <https://www.britannica.com/biography/Roy-Welensky>

systems they are fighting were embedded deep during the time of enslavement and in the process of colonization. It is like the back wheel of the bicycle trying to catch up with the front –our energy is spent on being the back wheel, but never quite getting there. Reflecting on this colonization, my mind fills with questions: *Who were the primitive ones? Who lacked wisdom? Who did not, and continues not, to understand the meaning of life and dignity?* Perhaps we need to reset the dial. To look closely and see what the benchmark of 'good' is, because it is surely not what we are following. What does our rich heritage tell us of what is good, what is wholesome and what is sustainable? My grandparents' stories, while a small piece in a larger narrative, provide for me an insight into what is.

ZAMU GURU NDEREKWAMAI –
THE BIGGER BREAST BELONGS TO THE MOTHER.

3

Peace and fire

In making the crossing, the Shona were running away from the serfdom of simply working for the White landlords in Southern Rhodesia. There they had been dispossessed of their land and stripped of their dignity, and there remained no real hope of having their own land. What did remain was the inner human silently contending with what was wrong and retaining what was right. This strong sense of justice was something Sekuru had in abundance.

The man I knew was a quiet peace maker, quite short, dark and with very distinctive features. Yet when you talk to those who knew him when he was younger, they will tell of his short and fiery temper. My mother once told me a story of her father losing his temper with his wife. *Sekuru* had been milking the cows and had filled several calabashes. As was the practice, my grandmother would follow him to collect the milk with the other women. However, on that day she was talking to her friends and didn't notice that the dog had started lapping up the milk from the calabash. When *Sekuru* noticed, he was livid! He kicked the calabashes and emptied the milk onto the ground until there was no milk for any of the meals that day. Apparently, he later apologized to all the women. Talk about cutting off your nose to spite your face! Yet when I talk to my mother, she says his temper was grounded in a strong sense of respect and a deep knowledge of what was just and what was not.

This same fire filled Sekuru one day as he watched his White boss whipping labourers on the farm. Sekuru thought it was excessive and mentioned it to his boss, who then told him to shut up or he would receive the same. Sekuru simply rolled up his sleeves and said, 'Bring it on. I will beat the living daylights out of you – and you can keep your job'. He was fearless and did not believe that any human being should be feared excessively. Luckily for Sekuru and his family, he was also a hard worker who delivered results; he kept his job.

I remember Sekuru, telling me that at one point in his life, like many other young men of his time, he had worked in the mines, but he had been discharged early because he suffered from asthma. With hindsight, I am not surprised, as one of the products being mined was asbestos. I wonder how many others were affected in a similar way, and whether nobody cared because they were dispensable? In spite of this physical limitation, Sekuru used his intellect and knowledge of gardening and farming and was never afraid of hard work.

It is that same hard work that saw him marry my grand-mother, Grace Madzibire, *mwana wekwa Sibanda* (a daughter from the Sibanda clan), who came from the same people as him, but was from Shurugwi, not too far from Gweru. It is said that Sekuru waited many years to marry her as he had to work for a long time to help his young brother find the money to pay 'damages' for having made a young woman pregnant, whom the brother later married. Then Sekuru had to work again to find the *lobola*, the bride price, for his own bride. Grace, known as *ma*Sibanda, later *mai* Juliet (mother of Juliet, because of her first-born daughter's name), or Mbuya by her grandchildren, who was an amazing person.

Mbuya was a very short woman whose physical features made me suspect that she might have had some heritage from among the *Basarwa* people of the then Bechuanaland (present day Botswana). She was also a very smart woman. She went to school at the Pakama mission in Southern Rhodesia until she was forced to withdraw. Her teacher, Mr Sithole, thought she had a lot of potential and approached her older brother, who was her guardian, to ask whether she could stay at his home and help look after his children as payment for board and lodging while she went to school. Her brother suspected that the teacher had other, more sinister reasons for wanting to help his young sister, and so he said no. Mbuya never went back to school, though by then she could already read and write quite well.

She was also known for her self-discipline. She once told me a story of her wedding day. In her village they would wed outside, the chairs being placed somewhere under a tree or where there was enough shade to ensure the bridal couple were comfortable. On this day, while the couple sat very quietly as expected, a lizard fell on to the bride and went inside her dress. Extraordinarily, she didn't jump or scream, but sat stoically as a well disciplined and well brought up young woman should (apparently). I am not sure I could have sat still! This discipline and self-control were visible to me and others. Mbuya managed the family while ensuring that everybody else believed they were in control.

Mbuya embodied unconditional love, which was modelled to me through her siblings. She had many brothers and, as she left Southern Rhodesia with Sekuru, her older brother asked three of his younger brothers to follow her and relocate with their families to live wherever Mbuya and Sekuru went to live to ensure that she was safe. This unconditional love was extended to Mbuya's children and grandchildren, and of course, Sekuru himself. He would often be heard advising young men of the importance of finding a good woman who was intelligent: '*Zamu guru nderekwamai*' he would say. Literally translated, 'the bigger breast belongs to the mother', but symbolically this was a reference to the great role that the mother and her family play in any child's life.

In addition to family members, they brought their material possessions with them to Northern Rhodesia, including their cattle. These were very important to them for many reasons, but primarily because of their centrality to peoples' livelihoods. They tilled the land, they used their milk, they provided meat; having cattle meant that families could feed themselves today and tomorrow. It was a form of investment, too, but here is where it gets all mixed up with some of the interpretations of custom and traditions regarding asset ownership and inheritance. Women were able to own cattle, or at least my Mbuya was. Apart from having three of her brothers follow her, Mbuya had also been given cattle by her brother, who wanted to ensure that there would always be milk for his nieces and nephews when they were born. Mbuya recalled that one of the cows she had was called *Gwanda*, who soon became a symbol of independence and love.

The woman's ownership of cattle would send an emphatic message that she came from a strong and loving family and was to be treated well and with respect. Gwanda must have died many years ago, but there was always the belief that of the cattle that belonged to Mbuya, in her later life, Gwanda's offspring were counted among them. Sekuru respected that right for Mbuya to own cattle; he had no authority over her property and only she could determine who would inherit the cattle, what they would be used for or when she would dispense with them. It was her decision to make, and when she passed, she made the final call on who would get what parts of her estate. She had written down her wishes and had shared them with one of her nephews; in death her wishes were respected. Such was the power and independence of the woman we called *Mbuya vama*Sibanda. We grew up with that lived experience of strong and respected women's voices.

Like many who made the crossing at the same time, my grandparents had dreams for their children, and their love was evident in how they worked hard to look after them, always treating them with fairness and encouragement. They wanted them to grow up, have families and be happy and well, instilling a strict work ethos in their children, particularly their two eldest girls. At a time when girls were seen as being of less value than boys, Sekuru believed that they should work as hard as any of the boys who came later, and be treated with the same respect. He didn't want them to be dependent on a man who may or may not treat them well. I remember him telling me that he sent my mother and her sister to school because he wanted to see his daughters do well. My mother went to Jean Rennie (now Kabulonga Girls Secondary School) in Lusaka. She was the first from her village to go to secondary school, and her father was very proud of her achievement. My mother tells stories of girls from White families who left the school to go to South Africa because they could not sit in the same classroom with children from the Black community. Her father paid £120 a year for her to be at the school – a hefty price for a Black farmer at the time. Yet he was committed to educating all his children, boys and girls. He was also able to influence his brother and brothers-in-law of the need for girls to be given equal opportunities, so almost all the girls in the village were sent to school. Despite this, not everyone did well there. Sometimes the schools were too far away to walk to daily, and so students stayed with family friends as boarders during school time, doing manual labour to help their host families as a form of payment. The girls were sometimes so exhausted from early morning chores that by the time they went to class, some would be falling asleep at their desks. My mother had first-hand experience of some of these hardships during her junior school, but still maintains that it helped make her stronger.

Sekuru fought for all the girls, not just his daughters. I remember one of my aunts from another branch of the family telling me that when she wanted to study nursing, her father refused and told her it was time to stay at home and find a husband. Sekuru intervened, and she was able to go and pursue a career as a nurse. Each time we saw her, she would remind us that, but for Sekuru's intervention, she would not have been who she became professionally. This was my first exposure to gender justice. I didn't understand the injustice at the time, but I took for granted the fact that all girls could go to school and be whatever they wanted to be. It was only later that I was to understand the patriarchal norms and practices that oppress women worldwide and among my own people.

It was not only in education that Sekuru was ahead of his time, he abhorred any form of domestic violence and was brave in fighting for what was fair and right. There was another older aunt, *ma*Moyo – the clan name used by my mother and all her cousins from her father's side of the family. She was the daughter of Sekuru's older brother from another mother (Sekuru came from a polygamous family; his mother was the fourth and youngest wife of *va*Mubambwe, who only had two children). My aunt had come over to live with Sekuru and went to school with my mother and her siblings, later marrying a Zambian man who used to beat her. After only nine months of this abusive marriage she sent word to Sekuru to inform him of her situation. What needed to be done was very clear in *Sekuru*'s mind and, as a man of action, he wasted no time at all. He went to collect her. The husband tried to protest and asked for his *lobola* back. Sekuru refused and told the man and his family that this was not a trade deal and that he would not allow any of his daughters to stay in an abusive relationship. He told them that if they were unhappy with that, they could take him to court. With those few words, he got his niece and went back home, where Sekuru defended and protected her from village 'displeasure'. My aunt divorced her husband, and many years later she married someone else.

We heard these stories as young girls playing at the feet of Mbuya. It was inevitable that these lessons would become embedded in our beliefs. We were encouraged to dream and be the best versions of ourselves.

ZVAKAFAMBA SEIKO VANHUWE? –
WHAT HAPPENED, PEOPLE?

4

The trees know my name

When my grandparents first arrived in Northern Rhodesia they settled in the central province in a place called Kwa James, now called Lusaka West. Back then, places were known by the name of the White farmers who 'owned' them. I place 'owned' in inverted commas because of the significance of the dispossession of the land by those who colonized Africa. This became the first but most critical way to take away the power of the people. Later in my life I would write a paper on the issue of land and sovereignty while studying at Warwick University. The fact that much land was not fairly acquired, and that the matter has never been adequately settled, remains a sore point that perpetuates injustice to this day. In many countries, the attitude has been to 'let bygones be bygones', but that in no way signifies a lack of consciousness of the issue. Like a small snake, such consciousness is burrowed deep inside the social fabric of society, and every so often when things break down, it rears its head and spits venom into the air, infecting and affecting everyone within reach who, in turn, responds with anger and outrage at the injustice of it all.

Kwa James was so named because the farm belonged to a White farmer called Mr James. The agreement was that Sekuru and others would work the land for the landowner and in turn they were given small patches of land on which to grow their own crops. They would harvest the owner's lands first, after which Mr James would invite them to glean the land and pick up any leftovers. Mr James would also collect about a tenth of the personal yield of the workers. Away from their native country and working for White farmers, they never forgot the reasons for their migrating. They kept focused on their dream to farm their own pieces of land and be independent. They banded together as families and communities and worked hard, they saved and they communicated well to ensure that knowledge of opportunities was shared. They also learned other ways of farming from the White farmers (and I believe the White farmers learnt from them too), and when they left Kwa James, they were able to find more permanent host communities, grow roots and grow their own wealth.

Sekuru and Mbuya went on to settle in a place called Mwalilanda just after Landless corner, off Kabwe road about 100km north as you come from Lusaka in Zambia. This was the land of the *Lenjes*, a people in the central province of Zambia on the way to the Copperbelt province. The local head man was called *ba*Mwalilanda. Each morning *ba*Mwalilanda would come to Mbuya's kitchen from his home and he would sit and have breakfast. Sekuru and Mbuya were nicknamed 'mupavose' because they 'gave to everyone'. They would take food to the widows and orphans and would always welcome those who did not have much.

The Shona migrants grew in strength and made an impact on the land and on the people that they found, working together as families and helping one another during planting and harvesting. They made a list of all the fields from the different families that needed planting or harvesting, then they made a schedule detailing the days and times at which they would all go to work on a specific field. After harvesting, they would celebrate together.

They were distinct from the indigenous people of their adopted country in many ways, as were their homesteads. Shona homes were big rotundas, but also rectangular and square. The roofs were made of dry grass or reeds neatly knitted together to form thatch in a style known as 'matiki', and then lifted up and placed on top of the clay walls. The walls themselves would be painted with drawings of animals, plants and at times geometric designs. The floors would be made with clay and sand. I remember as a child being asked to help out with protecting the floor from cracks and dust. We used cow dung to cover the floor and, once it was dry, we took a flat stone and 'shined' the floor. This sealed the small cracks in the floor and ensured that it was smooth and without dust from the mud floor. We all played a valuable part in the home and learned by observing and practising what we were taught.

Beyond the homestead, we also helped out in the fields. My grandfather would point out trees and explain their nature and their importance; some were used for medicinal purposes, but all were worth looking after. My mother shared with me a story that Sekuru told her one day when they were walking back to the village after visiting some relatives. She was just a young girl, but it is a story that has become increasingly important to me throughout my life and I have embraced it as my own.

It had been raining heavily and as they walked, the place was still and quiet. The storm had shaken some of the branches from the trees, which were beginning to drop. When they did, a large cracking sound filled the air and my mother was scared.

'Don't to be afraid,' Sekuru would say, 'the trees are talking about you. They are wondering what your name is. One tree says to the other, "She is called Juliet". The other says, "No". The first tree says, "I will call her name and you will see that she will jump…"'

'And so,' Sekuru would go on, 'wherever you go, you must always remember that the trees and the earth know who you are. So, if you forget who you are, just remember what I have told you and you will be fine.'

This story has been told several times, so that it has become almost like folklore, with a girl walking with her father or grandfather. When I tell this story it is my story, and I hear my grandfather talking to me and the trees calling my name. Although at the time I was too young to appreciate the significance of what he was saying, eventually I would come to understand.

I recently went back to the village to visit the *hama* who still live there. As we walked to the burial site with family members, I could not help but notice how barren the land looked. With years of climate change it was very hot and dry, the soil looked more like sand than a place where crops could grow and water remain. And the trees that Sekuru had talked about, the trees that knew my name? They're now gone. Looking around me I felt a sense of loss filling my heart.

If the trees are gone, does it mean that the earth does not know me anymore? There is no breeze, just dry and hot air. I can't see the birds either, those little sounds I used to hear as a child. Those sounds represented life in all its diversity, I can hardly hear them.

'What happened to the trees?' I asked those with me.

'Ah, the trees, they were cut down.'

'But why?' I asked.

'*Aah, chibili kaili,*' they explained – the trees were used to make charcoal to sell, it was the only way to generate income. I noticed that even the language had changed, now you could hear a mixture of Shona, Lenje and Nyanja.

'*Asi, miti yose sure? Matamba, Muchakata zvose?*' I asked. I thought we were not allowed to cut down fruit trees that grew in the wild? '*Michero yemusango?*' Weren't we told that these trees were sacred, did not belong to any one person, provided food and therefore should never be cut down?

'*Zvakafamba seiko vanhuwe?*' I asked. What happened, people? I couldn't understand what had changed.

'*Aah, mari kaili,*' they replied – money.

I looked on at the wilderness space, feeling the wilderness in my soul. The *Mutondo* and the *Musasa* trees, the buck of which has been used for knitting reed mats and thatched roofs for generations – all gone. *Muwonde, Musekese* trees used to alert the community to potential water sources – all gone. It was heartbreaking. Sekuru and his peers had a great respect for the unwritten rules around the environment. Each tree had a name and purpose in the circle of life. Each animal had a role to play in keeping the planet working and every bird of the air had its own significance. Humans had both the power to be wise and the responsibility to ensure that the planetary balance was kept. 'Eat what you need and leave the rest,' was what we heard all the time.

The generation that understood the good 'taboos' around living in harmony with the environment had all but disappeared. Driven by changing consumption habits and where money is king, everything has a price and is up for sale. You can smell the land's devastation. Deforestation is everywhere and the community now cries out for the rain and for fertile land. They don't see the role they have played in destroying the land that fed their ancestors before them.

Visiting the burial site brought it home for me; we had lost more than grandparents. We had lost our humility. Our arrogance will come at a cost. In all their search for greener pastures, they never lost their understanding of a universe that was interdependent. They understood that their survival depended upon living in harmony with others, with the animals and with the earth. Yet somehow, did they fail to pass this knowledge, love and respect to their descendants?

VANA VAMABWIDI –
CHILDREN OF FOREIGNERS.

5

Then the singing stopped

For some the Shona are known for their direct approach – they spoke candidly on difficult issues based on their own experiences of dealing with those who had oppressed them. Yet for me, they were a people with music in their heart. Their love for singing brought them together to share and celebrate and to ensure that we knew one another.

They would sing during harvest; they would sing during planting season; and most of all, they would sing during weddings. They would also pass on knowledge through song. They would sing of their homeland. I remember a song '*Kure ku musha, Habana ye, Habana ye, Salisbury, Salisbury ye*' (home is far, Salisbury, Salisbury is far), which my uncles would sing while pointing to some faraway place. We would sing of the role of our mothers and Mbuyas, that they had a big job to do in the family, and so we would pray that *Mwari*, God, would give them long lives and strength to look after us (*Ava amai vedu vatinavo pano, mwana wekwa Moyo vane basa guru. Kumbirayi tsitsi kuna Mwari BaBa kuti avape masimba makuru*). We would name them and their parentage as we sung. I learned all the names of my mother's siblings and the hierarchy according to birth through songs.

I loved the singing. It was not sanitized, but as with many things from this community, the singing was filled with the imperfections and emotions of the people. I love African voices lifted in song, the way they harmonize and come together. I can't say it enough. It would be through music that I would hear the voice of God speaking to me and calling me to give my life to His service. In singing, messages beyond normal words would be conveyed. We would hear joy, sadness, anguish and jubilation, depending on the circumstances. In my own home, especially when my children were little, I too would break into song to express my happiness, joy or doubt. Yet still, it never compared to the singing I grew up with; they sang with soul.

Then the singing changed. In the 1970s, the music moved from cries of celebration to words of war and fighting. The liberation struggle for Southern Rhodesia was going on and the people fighting for freedom had become more militant. Sekuru and Mbuya's village in Zambia became a refuge for the freedom fighters from both ZANU and ZAPU. When they passed by, they would be given sanctuary for a while. When the time came for them to move on, they would be given bags of maize and other food. Sekuru was very committed to helping the liberation struggle and the 'children' who had gone to fight the war. The freedom fighters would recruit from the Shona and Ndebele communities – they would look for young men and women to go and join the Chimurenga movement.

Those young men and women who remained learned the freedom songs and brought the words and tunes into our social spaces. The dancing changed as well, and the *toyi toyi* (the exercise that the freedom fighters used to keep fit as they sang war songs) began to permeate through wedding and celebration songs and dance routines. Yet throughout, the same ideals and values of hard work and discipline would be at the fore. Through music they shared a dream with their children, a dream for something we didn't quite understand, but knew was good because our people sang of it and tried to touch it with their voices. It was elusive. I have never been able to quite put my hand around it and name it, but now I think it was trying to reach for freedom, for dignity and for wellbeing. It left you feeling like you were wandering in the wilderness trying to get home.

Then the singing stopped. There was a dearth of song and a desert of silence. Occasionally you would hear someone singing, but it was no longer about home and it was no longer soulful. When I look back, I think it was a time when the light of hope faded until you could barely see it. Maybe it was, once the struggle for Zimbabwe's independence had been won. Those who wanted to go back had left, and those who remained were trying to disappear into the host communities. They went underground, running away from fear of silent persecution in the form of exclusion from employment and public services and the stigma of being a migrant. The price they had to pay for remaining and integrating in their host communities was the loss of their voice and, ultimately, of their identity. It was a heavy price to pay and would impact upon the generations to come. Even as they integrated, they ensured that their values and ethos of hard work stayed with them, but the cracks of integration had started separating the young from the old – those who made the crossing from those who were born in Zambia.

As the children of these immigrants grew up and started their own families, they inter-married with the indigenous population of Northern Rhodesia, or Zambia as it was called by this time, and raised their own families. They seemingly integrated very well, but the reality was different. I remember we were called derogatory names as children, referred to as *vana vamaBwidi*, meaning children of foreigners, but it also used to imply a primitive people. The Shona settlers considered the host communities to be lazy, ill-disciplined and lacking in determination to achieve success. The offspring of such inter-marriages became easy targets for insult by the settlers. What the settlers came to learn much later was the varied values that different groups bring to community life. The host communities were initially generous and welcoming, they shared their land and gave the settlers fields in which to grow their crops, burial sites for their dead and land to build their homes on. Yet the settlers were arrogant at first, blind to this kindness. You don't come into somebody's home and start treating them badly – that is essentially what the settlers did.

If a Shona man married from outside their ethnic group, their spouse would have to integrate fully – their women had to all but erase all characteristics of their people. Shona and Ndebele women would marry outside their community and would be expected to teach their children their ways of life and their values. So whichever way, for the majority, if one of your parents was from among the Shonas, you grew up with more knowledge of Shona values than anything else. At the same time, you knew that the community would be more accepting of you if you were more Zambian than foreigner. And so the struggle within would rage on as young adults tried to understand their environment and yet survive in a country that had become hostile to these foreigners, which meant subverting those visible aspects of Shona heritage.

As for me, my father was an immigrant from the then Nyasaland, now Malawi. He was a Ngoni man who had come to work in the armed forces in Zambia. He was the first Black band master for the Zambian Army. He trained at Kneller Hall, at the Royal Military School of Music, in the late 1960s, and it was in that period that I was born in Twickenham, Middlesex. He died in Zambia when I was very young. I later visited Kneller Hall in my adulthood, it was quite an emotional experience. I had heard stories of his musical career in the band, but as I looked around and had a drink in a nearby pub where he likely socialized with his colleagues, I was seeing first-hand evidence that he had existed.

Though his family did not have much direct influence on me, my mother wanted us to have some understanding of our paternal heritage, and so she made it her business to instil in us what she saw as my father's values . We came from the clan of the eagle, and saw ourselves as being as strong as the eagle. She made sure that while there was a gap in physical connection with the family, we still shared the same values and ideals. Amazingly, many years later as adults, when I encountered my father's people for the first time, the shared values and beliefs were very clear – *strong and humble, education is key, faith is paramount.*

Back then, my mother knew that at some point, knowledge of our father and his values, his people and his dreams would be important for us as we tried to understand ourselves. It was not only that she was politically and socially astute, she came from a patrilineal ethnic group and understood that, in terms of identity, we would never be fully accepted as 'children' of the Shona. We would always be seen and welcomed as children of the daughters (grandchildren of the family) of the Shona, rather than children of sons (children of the family). The difference is subtle, but important. Children have rights within the group. Children have authority and power within the group, even though female children have fewer rights than male. Grandchildren born from a female child do not have the same rights and authority. While they loved and cared for their daughter's or sister's children, when push came to shove, those nieces or nephews did not have the power that came with assets, voice and inheritance. Those children born to their sister were not Shona. I was not Shona. Therefore, there was no seat for me within the inner circle of identity, within the decision-making circle.

As a young child, this reality did not have too much impact on me, or perhaps I was not as aware of it. I lived in two worlds: one was indoors where everything that was Shona ruled – from cultural norms and practices to the language, there was nothing in my behaviour inside the home that suggested I had any other heritage but Shona. The other world was outside the home. Fluent in Nyanja, I was a child being raised in the suburbs of a growing capital city. Oblivious to the struggle of bringing together these two worlds, I neither saw nor experienced any challenges. Compartmentalization worked quite well. I, perhaps like many others in my generation, learned to keep the two worlds separate and, for a while, it worked well. Then we grew up, became aware, wanted voice, wanted space. We wanted to be seen and acknowledged.

I needed to change this reality. My ability to influence or shape any decisions within the Shona side of the family came as a result of knowledge of the people, the practices and the greater context outside of the community. The power to speak, to influence and to be listened to came from my mother's commitment to educate us. Education as in going to school to get better access to knowledge; education as in exposure to different people and cultures; education about our paternal identity and heritage. I needed to make sense of my identity as *mwana wemuBwidi*, the child of two foreigners, a Shona and a Ngoni. Yet our reality was about to change again.

CHISINGAPERI CHINOSHURA, CHINOKWEGURA CHINOKOTAMA·

Musoro wegudo chave chinokoro.
*What does not end is taboo, what grows must bend,
the head of a monkey has become a spoon.*

6

Growing pains

Chisingaperi chinoshura, chinokwegura chinokotama,
musoro wegudo chave chinokoro.
What does not end is taboo, what grows must bend, the
head of a monkey has become a spoon.

Shortly before Northern Rhodesia gained independence
in 1964 and became known as Zambia, there was a difficult
period. The White farmers and others who could not fathom a
life where Blacks and Whites lived side by side as equal human
beings (the majority) sold up and left. My grandfather Sekuru
was offered a farm for £2 and turned it down. Instead, he
started his own small but lucrative farm. Bhudhii Silandeni
was offered the opportunity to travel to England to train as a
Methodist preacher, because he had learned some English and
was deemed to have some intelligence to master the training.
He too turned the offer down in favour of staying with Sekuru
and Mbuya. Suffice it to say, their lives would have turned out
differently if they had taken these paths, and there were others
who accepted such lucrative offers.

One of the younger men who came with Sekuru and
Mbuya from the then Southern Rhodesia accepted a farm.
With hard work and dedication, he kept it as a successful
business, teaching his children, both male and female, how to
run a farming business. Today, they all have very successful

43

farming businesses of their own. I always thought of Sekuru and Mbuya's refusal as missed opportunities, yet this opinion is filtered through dominant and mainstream narratives, looking at prosperity as it has now been defined by a capitalist ideology. When I try and think differently, I wonder whether they opted for a more humane lifestyle with enough to live on while being happy, their dignity intact and spirit protected from eternal greed.

Southern Rhodesia was still a British colony. In the 1970s, the struggle for independence from the British was reaching its height, with freedom fighters seeking refuge in several southern and eastern African countries such as Zambia, Mozambique and Tanzania. Freedom fighters in Zambia were targeted with bombings by the Ian Smith and Muzorewa regimes of Southern Rhodesia. Innocent Zambians died and many were injured in the process. In the meantime, the then President of Zambia, Kenneth Kaunda, pursued a foreign policy that was focused on helping other African countries to be free from colonial rule. As a landlocked country, dependent upon neighbouring countries to get to the sea for trade, Zambia experienced economic hardship because of its foreign policy position. It was the right thing to do, but it cost the Zambian government a lot of money and the Zambian people their livelihoods. As so often happens in these situations, Zambians turned on the settlers, accusing them of taking their jobs, their land and their businesses. Further, upon Zambia's independence, the government wanted to ensure that its people had access to education and employment, taking over all the jobs that they had hitherto been denied. There was no room for foreigners.

For the settlers, their experience of their newfound home turned sour, and those who could find new identities among the local communities began to change their names and backgrounds. They dropped their typical and easily identifiable Zimbabwean names and adopted Zambian ones instead: a Sibanda became a Banda, Ndhlovu became a Njovu, others became Tembos, Moyos easily became Moyos from the eastern province of Zambia, or Mooyos from the southern province, and so on. With a Shona name, it became difficult to obtain formal employment or be easily accepted. The Zambian government had instituted a process of issuing identity cards to all inhabitants of Zambia. If you were Zambian, then you would carry a green card. If you were a foreigner, then you would be given a pink card. You had to have these cards on you all the time and be prepared to produce them on demand.

The generation born in Zambia found it difficult; their Zimbabwean identity became a burden, and for some this was too much, so they shed it altogether and assimilated into local ethnic groups, traditions and practices. *Ndiri muRenje*, meaning 'I am Lenje', is a phrase that a number of Zambians with Zimbabwean heritage whose families lived in the central province of Zambia will understand. Unable to pronounce the L in Lenje properly, the settlers would try to say they were of the Lenje ethnic group. Those with Zambian fathers were able to navigate the social, economic and political spaces, but it was at the expense of diminishing your maternal heritage, at least the visible elements of it such as language.

As the conflict in Zimbabwe raged on, with Ian Smith acting as lord of the manor – refusing to let go and fighting to stay at the top of the food chain in a land that was not legitimately his, with resources that did not belong to him – the space for the economic migrants in Zambia was shrinking. There was nowhere to run to. Some chose to erase their heritage, others decided to simply hide it, while others decided they would stand firm and true to who they were. The truth is that none of these groups were wrong or right, it was a question of what strategy to use to protect yourself, your family and your community – a question of survival. As for me, there was nowhere to run. As my father had died early on in our lives, Shona was the only ethnic group we really understood – the Shona community was our community and our family were the Shona people.

At the height of the Zimbabwean struggle, uncles and aunts would sit and discuss what would happen next. Some planned to go back 'home', others wanted to stay. My mother was asked by the late freedom fighter Tongogara, who was close to her and her family, to go to Mozambique and join the struggle in exile, but she decided that she was home already. Zambia was where she wanted to be, so she would stay –she was Zambian. When asked about her decision, she gives two key reasons: first, her parents, who were still alive at the time, had settled in Zambia; secondly, to go with Tongogara, she would have had to leave her children with her parents. At the time of her marriage, she had lived in the UK and so had broadened her own dreams of the life she wanted for her children, and it was not to grow up in the village. She chose to stay and raise her girls there and, for that, I am grateful.

It was a traumatic time for the Shona. I remember as a child being told that we might have to go on the run. I couldn't remember all the details, so I asked my mother. It was in 1978, she told me. Ian Smith had bombed two places in Lusaka, one near the State House. He was looking for Joshua Nkomo, who had been given refuge by the Zambian government. You could see the smoke from where we lived. My mother thought she should get us ready to run, so she dressed us up in several dresses and a pair of trousers each, packed some light bags and waited. Her young brother encouraged her instead to stay quietly in the house and wait it out. A curfew and a blackout had been put in place by the government to stop the Smith regime from finding their targets. The freedom fighters were accommodated within the communities.

In the morning there were army personnel all over the place, there to protect the people, but I still felt afraid. My mother's people, the Karangas, were a particularly interesting group among the Shona who didn't believe in what they saw as cosseting a child. They were straight-talkers, and as such there wasn't much sympathy for what was seen as self-pity. There was no sugar-coating of difficult subjects, you were given direct feedback no matter how hard it was, and you were expected to digest it, grow up and move on. You learned to handle conflict. You took sides – there were no observers and being on the fence was not encouraged. I learned to speak my mind. I learned to confront. I learned to stand my ground. And so, when our young faces looked up to our parents with questions of 'What now?', the answer we often got back was, 'It is what it is. Live with it.' So we pushed back the fear and soldiered on.

As the independence of Zimbabwe loomed, my mother's best friend packed her bags and, with her children, went back to the new Zimbabwe. Families were split as brothers and sisters went to vote in the first elections in Southern Rhodesia and took different sides, very much along ethnic lines. I overheard a couple of my uncles from the extended family arguing about whether to go and vote for ZANU PF or ZAPU. One party was led by Joshua Nkomo from the Ndebeles, the other was led by Robert Mugabe from the Shona. My uncles were Shona, and the expectations were that they would go and vote for Mugabe. One of the uncles insisted that he was going to vote for Nkomo. This was a betrayal. This uncle of mine and his father travelled together to go to Zimbabwe to vote. They voted for different parties and sadly, as a result, travelled back separately, never speaking again. My uncle died before his father and, on his death bed, his father came to see him and simply said *kuyafa lokhu*, meaning 'this one is dying'. Such was the depth of emotion and, dare I say, irrationality. We learned something from this experience – politics should never be allowed to be king. It is made by the people and should be managed by people.

WE KNOW
THAT THERE IS
SOMETHING THAT
WE SHARE THAT
GOES BEYOND
THE CURRENT
BOUNDARIES OF
OUR COUNTRIES.

7

The new Zambia and Zimbabwe

After the independence of Zimbabwe in 1980, there was a mass exodus of Shona settlers from Zambia going back to Zimbabwe. There were expectations and excitement among them. One of my uncles decided to go back. The people who went were mainly those who had never lived in Zimbabwe, but because of the experience they had in Zambia, they felt they would be more welcome at 'home' where they belonged ... or so they thought.

The Zimbabwe they found was different to that they had heard of. The war had left many problems; the struggle had changed people. For those who chose to remain in Zambia and for the Zambians more generally, there was a sense of sadness and anger. Zimbabwe, as would South Africa in future, forgot the sacrifice of its neighbours. They forgot those who gave them shelter when they needed it.

This continues to this day, and the impact of this narrative on those Shona who remained in Zambia contributed to the loss of identity and voice they experienced and continue to experience to this day. When Zambia went through its economic hardships in the late 1980s and early 1990s, Zimbabwe was unhelpful to Zambia. Little did the Zimbabweans know that worse was to come for them, and that they would need their neighbours once again. The Mugabe regime was filled with great disappointment.[6] Zimbabweans would flee the country in droves to go and search for a more dignified life. They flooded neighbouring countries in their millions, going to Zambia, Botswana, South Africa and, those who could afford it, moving to Europe, Australia and many other countries.

For those of us whose parents chose to be Zambians, one is left with an inner struggle between the sacrifice that Zambians made and the shame that you felt because of the perceived ingratitude of Zimbabwe. History has not captured the details of this struggle well, the knowledge has not been passed on and mistakes continue to be repeated. While Western countries come together on a regular basis to remind one another of the sacrifices they have made together, this is not the case with Zimbabwe, and now with South Africa and the role of the frontline states in their emancipation. The current persecution of other Africans in South Africa is a shocking and poor indictment of the people and leaders (both past and present) of South Africa. In addition, their seemingly lack of appreciation of a one-Africa concept for the survival and prosperity of the continent, is very disappointing and is something that they will need to comprehend at some point in their development, especially if they are to be as great a country and leader as they can potentially be. The only excuse is perhaps that these countries are not yet settled. The struggle for their heritage, their identity and for their dignity continues. That's how I square the circle.

We are now adults with families of our own and we too

---

6   Robert Mugabe was President of Zimbabwe for 34 years.

are travelling the world, searching for economic prosperity and wellbeing. That sense of wandering in the wilderness has not left, so we continue searching and learning. As we begin to interact with those from Zimbabwe who remained there during the struggle and who have now also moved to other countries in the West, we realize that we are different. The values and ideals that were passed on to us have evolved and changed among both those who left and those who remained in Zimbabwe.

The experiences of the two groups are very different. The struggles are also different, both then and now. For those who left, their values have been passed onto our generation, placed into a melting pot of other values coming from different ethnic groups, different lives and different stories. Those who remained had some respite for a little while, when they thought independence would bring political and economic freedoms and wellbeing and dignity for all Zimbabweans. But it was just for a little while.

That economic and political freedom, the enjoyment of dignity and wellbeing, has remained out of reach of this young nation. The pain of the struggle at the hands of those you regard as your own people has scattered the people to the different parts of the world. Almost like the 'great scattering' of 1821, the *Mfecane* – which in Nguni means 'crushing' – is the name given to the period of a forced migration among indigenous ethnic communities in southern Africa, which is speculatively attributed to a range of reasons, such as fleeing from war, drought and other distress. This present-day movement has its roots in economic injustice, political turmoil and intolerance, and has lasted for many decades with no visible end in sight. The stories of what has happened, like so many others throughout history, have been confused over time. Historically, the people who 'scattered' used oral traditions to pass on stories, much of which was lost or misinterpreted by European writers – including 'White missionaries, travellers and government officials.'[7] Now we must tell and write stories of our own truths.

The new Zimbabwe is a social construct that we do not know, understand nor relate to. Yet we find links, connections and meeting points. We know there is something that we share which goes beyond the current boundaries of our countries. We know that at one point in our past, our ancestors shared the same values, villages and dreamed the same dreams. The concept of nationhood that predates the division of Africa is truly lost. It continues to hurt the politics, the social and economics of the continent. While I am a product of two great nations and peoples, the boundaries of Zambia, Zimbabwe and Malawi have created divisions that don't make sense. The nations of people transcend these boundaries. It is a lost heritage that we must strive to rediscover and reclaim before it's too late.

Mbuya has now passed on. There is nothing left of Gwanda. Her house in the village has been abandoned and there is nobody there any longer. Like Sekuru, she died as a permanent resident in Zambia with her pink national registration card (given to foreigners in Zambia), despite having lived there for over 60 years and being entitled to full citizenship. I am left wondering whether this was a symbol

---

7   <https://www.sahistory.org.za/article/political-changes-1750-1835>

of resistance, but it was definitely an expression of self-awareness and identity. While in practice they understood that the national borders were a political gimmick meant to satisfy the interests of something beyond their control, they nevertheless respected the laws, regulations and customs of their hosts. They learned from them and also contributed to the learning and livelihoods of their host communities. They are buried with the unwritten label *baswamashi* – foreigners – on land kindly provided by the Lenje people in Keembe in the central province of Zambia.

The villages of the Shona people who settled in Zambia have also been slowly diminishing and are being abandoned. You can see those that remain, still identifiable from afar because of the signature thatched roofs. Whereas before villages were very different to towns, now the town has come to the villages and the countryside has lost its soul. There has been massive urban migration and the few people who have remained in rural areas are losing their relationship with the land and to be custodians of what is good and whole. They now depend upon bread from the cities, on sugar, on harmful drinks and everything that we have defined as a sign of development and progress. There is no longer any focus on caring for the environment. Instead, people aspire for the city.

We have lost something precious in that we always had two homes, one home in the city and another at the village. We were proud to spend time in both places, we could survive in either. It was about being grounded in kith and kin. Yet that love for the land has gone from the people. I still have a few uncles in the village, but I wonder how long I will continue to go there. The descendants have many heritages, have moved to urban areas or settled in other lands. It feels sad, but it should not.

I went back to the village to bury Mbuya. It was an amazing experience. It has changed, but people are singing again and with great harmony. I cannot quite pinpoint what has changed in the music, but I think it has new elements in the rhythm. There is more clapping as people sing, and faster steps. The soullessness has left the music. It is a music that speaks of a different identity, an evolved identity that sings a different song. It is not a song of sadness, but of newness. The singing is now a mixture of different values, pieces and identities.

I watched my aunts dancing and singing as they mourned for a mother gone, the last of the elders. The closing of a village. There were at least a thousand people there, about the same number that had attended her husband's funeral all those years back. They came from near and far. It spoke of the force that this couple had been; it pointed to a life of caring and sharing, one of humility. It showed what can be achieved when one embraces others rather than excludes them. The people who came for the funerals came because they had different touch points with Sekuru and Mbuya. They made the journey to bid farewell to a loved couple who had, at one time or another, embraced them or members of their family or community in a very real way. The message was clear, Sekuru and Mbuya had touched people's lives in ways that one can only dream of. This was the end of an era.

Seventy years after the migration of Shona settlers from what is now Zimbabwe into Zambia began, I know this much: they have been enriched by the new communities of which they became part, and their host communities have also been enriched by them. Today, there is only one community, and it is a new creation with a new relationship, made up of multiple pieces that are different. As long as they continue to evolve, they will continue to live. They cannot go back because there is nothing there. They can only move forward and walk the uncharted path. They can do this with a new dance, new music, a new song.

THE SINGING SPOKE TO THE VERY DEPTHS OF THE SOUL.

8

Found by faith

There are things that come across your path and at the time, you may not realize it, but they become important to you on your journey. Faith was mine – it found me and changed me. My early experiences of faith were varied. Where Mbuya was God-fearing and a self-professed Christian, Sekuru was, at best, agnostic, but otherwise a non-believer in what he saw as the White man's god. He believed there was a higher divine deity called *Mwari*, it was clear that Mwari was god of everyone and for everyone, that Mwari would choose to give as he wanted. He was also not a great follower of ancestral worship.

I remember once, when one of my uncles was very ill, a traditional ceremony was held for him to find out from the ancestral spirits what was wrong, and what the cure might be. The women brewed traditional beer made from millet, the drummers came and the dancing took place. Sekuru wore the *magagada*, a traditional dance artefact made with small calabashes tied together and then worn around each calf. When he danced, they jangled. He was very good and had great rhythm. I remember him telling me that he danced because he enjoyed the drums, not because he believed that someone would come from the dead, from among the fallen ancestors to provide answers. He preferred the ancestors solve their own problems and leave the living to get on with the business of living.

In so far as Christianity is concerned, while Sekuru didn't criticize it as a belief system and was respectful of those who believed, he stayed away from Christian rituals. Interestingly, some of their children went the Christian route and others fell in between, straddling both Christian and ancestral heritage. It's interesting, because present day Christianity has adopted traditions from different cultures around the world – those from the west are more acceptable than those from developing countries. For example, Christmas is not a biblical feast or celebration, yet it is now taken as read that it is a Christian festival, because it is in honour of the birth of Jesus Christ. However the tree, Santa, crackers and the Christmas turkey are all adopted from local traditions in Europe. While it is acceptable to pray for all the departed souls as part of the Christian ritual, it is less acceptable to commune with the ancestors, as is the custom among some groups in Africa. I don't think Sekuru had analysed Christianity, but what he understood was enough to keep him steadfast with his beliefs as well as to support Mbuya in hers.

Mbuya and my mother have always been women of great faith in Jesus. They have stood firm by the word of God. Mbuya loved singing and all her songs were of praise and worship. She praised God when she was happy, she praised God when she was sad. My mother converted to Catholicism when she was married and raised us, her children, as Catholics. I remember receiving my First Holy Communion in Makeni, a residential area in Lusaka. I must have been about 10 or 11 years old. A mass service for the area was organized, and I remember having to do my first confession to our local Priest, Father Gastone. I had no clue what I was doing, I just remember feeling that I had to make up some sins to confess! Then the choirs from the different churches came to sing. I cannot begin to describe the sound of singing that would emerge when everyone came together; it spoke to the very depths of the soul.

We moved to Italy soon after that. My mother had re-married and my stepfather was sent to the diplomatic service to Rome. While there, I was exposed to a more intense form of Catholicism – it was everywhere. I was confirmed in Rome by one of the cardinals. I think that as a young girl, together with my siblings, we did not comprehend fully the privilege of being in this wonderful city and in such proximity to the Vatican City. It was here, around the age of 17, where I started thinking about my own relationship with God and all that that entails.

I was at school in Rome where my stepfather had been working as a Zambian diplomat. At the end of my penultimate year of secondary school, my parents were transferred from Italy to Ethiopia. Wanting to ensure that we were not too disturbed at school, I was left with a family friend in Rome to complete my sixth form. With this new-found freedom, one would expect that I would have embraced and enjoyed it. It didn't work out quite like that.

The first thing I had to learn to do was attend the home office for a change in visa status. Eish! I showed up at the Home Office at about ten in the morning, but little did I realize that with places like that, you need to show up very early – very, very early. I was not seen on that day. I had to come back another day, and this time I was there early, by six, and in the queue. I started growing up and it was during this period that I first attended Baptist church with an American family who lived in the same area and whose children went to the same school as me. I listened to the preaching and Bible studies and really loved the times that I spent with the church community, meeting some young college students who loved God. People were very warm and kind. I heard many testimonies of living with Christ. But time was going quickly, and soon it was time for me to go home to my parents in Ethiopia, and from there I went to Zambia for university.

I was still searching for a spiritual home, although at the time I was not able to articulate it quite so succinctly. I continued to attend the Catholic church at the university. To start with, it was very much a matter of routine, but I was committed. It felt like the right thing to do. I was given responsibilities and I started to search the scriptures. The University of Zambia is home to many different denominations and, as a student, one tends to be inquisitive. I was no exception and I got into many discussions with others on what the Bible said about different things.

During one short break, I visited my mother's brother who lived in Lusaka. His wife was a member of the Seventh Day Adventist Church. One evening she asked if I could go with her to attend a funeral; a young girl had died while trying to light a fire at home. I went with my aunt to the funeral house and, while she sat inside the house, which was very small, I sat outside with other young people there. As was and perhaps still is, common at funerals in Zambia, there were several choirs taking turns to sing and pray. A small acapella group called 'The Revelators' got up to sing. They sang several very uplifting songs, one of which proved a turning point for me. Singing in Bemba, one of the Zambian languages, the song was a call for people to answer Jesus as He knocked at the door. It was so real and it touched me; I wanted to hear more such songs and asked my aunt; she invited me to go to her church and hear the group sing. I went and listened, sitting with some of the group members and studying the Bible together. I asked questions and read the scriptures for myself, searching through my spiritual wilderness.

I wanted to have a personal relationship with Jesus and God. So slowly, I searched for answers and found them in the word of God. I was about 20 years old at the time. I chose to be baptized in the Seventh Day Adventist Church in 1989, and since then I have tried to find my own way among the myriad of thoughts and views in the Church, from the most liberal to the most conservative. I became grounded in the word of God and excited that I could build that personal relationship with Him.

This grounding would come to serve me well in the years when I moved to the UK. At the same time as I found my faith, I also started to awaken from my slumber on issues of social justice.

FIGHTING FOR SOCIAL JUSTICE WAS THE RIGHT THING TO DO, A MUST-DO FOR ALL HUMAN BEINGS.

9

Awakening my consciousness

Returning home to Zambia from Ethiopia was a surreal period, but it was about to become the making of me. My experience during my years at university proved a steep learning curve and would leave a transformative mark on my consciousness forever.

The years 1987–1991 were the height of the transition for Zambia's politics and, in my view, the University of Zambia became the heart of the fight against political and economic injustice. The students there came from all walks of life, with the shared objective of gaining an education that would open doors to an improved quality of life for them and their families. Some families sacrificed a lot to ensure that the one child who had successfully qualified could actually travel to the university and attend. A child going to university and moving away from home for some families meant a labour gap in farming, lower production and less income to feed the family. Government bursaries ensured that all qualified students were able to take up that opportunity, have accommodation, be able to feed themselves and buy books. There was a kind of level playing field once you arrived at the university.

The university was a real centre of intellectual stimulation and freedom of thought. The School of Humanities and Social Sciences was particularly exciting, as it helped students explore and interrogate norms and practices that governed economic, political and social life in Zambia. Before long, my consciousness was awakened to all sorts of injustices in the systems: gender inequality, tribal injustice, patriarchy, imperialism, economic injustice. These began to shape my thoughts and positions and soon I was finding my voice.

In my last year at university, Nelson Mandela was released from prison after 27 years. His very first visit outside South Africa was to Zambia, just 16 days after his release. Zambia had been the headquarters of the African National Congress outside of South Africa and had played an incredible role in the liberation struggles of neighbouring countries. Nelson Mandela's visit to Lusaka was therefore a huge endorsement and recognition of Zambia's support and role in the South African struggle against apartheid. Yet while Zambia had a fantastic record of fighting injustice outside of the country, internally people were struggling. The one-party state had failed to deliver development for all its citizens; power was centralized; households struggled with poverty. The ordinary person was left out in the cold. There was political agitation for a multi-party democratic system of politics.

Students at the University of Zambia were central in analyzing decisions, interrogating actions of leadership and agitating for change. 'Forum, forum, forum,' you would hear students going from building to building calling us all to gather in an evening. The university was closed several times during the years I was there due to civil disobedience by students and, in my last year (1990–1991), the tension was palpable. Out of all the meetings that Nelson Mandela could have attended, one of them was an address to the University of Zambia students at their Lusaka campus. I was there among them. What a moment. What an experience. I remember the euphoria; here was a symbol of resistance, someone who had dedicated their life to fighting injustice, and he chose to come and speak to us at a time when we were most unhappy and fighting our own injustice. It was an extraordinary moment that crystallized my emerging conviction that fighting for social justice was the right thing to do, a must-do for all human beings. It would be the only way that the checks and balances of human behaviours and greed could be controlled. It was not a job for someone else, but a duty for each of us to tackle in different ways as we journey through life.

The following few years marked significant political change in Zambia. The new politics raised expectations, but alas, it was short-lived and the promises remained unfulfilled. Tribal politics returned into play, corruption reared its ugly head. Structural adjustment programmes sent working class households into despair. Political opponents were targeted. National companies were liquidated, creating unprecedented levels of unemployment. Perhaps what captures the mood and lived realities of many at the time was the banner held up at the airport by the late Lucy Banda-Sichone, as President Chiluba returned from a foreign trip: 'Welcome to Zambia; Our own Sharpeville massacre'.[8] People left the country. We left. I left.

I left behind my job with the Common Market for Eastern and Southern Africa, where I developed my understanding of women's rights and gender equality. The work on building women's economic empowerment, interrogating cross-border

---

8   Grieve Chelwa, 2015, 'Lucy Sichone – Conscience of the Zambian Nation', africas-country.com

legislation and practices that hindered women's access to markets, I also left behind. The work with women working in the informal sector, the work with women's struggles, I had to leave all this behind. Being able to interact with young people, orphans and vulnerable children left behind by the devastation caused by HIV and Aids at the time, I choose to give up. Being able to sit with the elderly as they told their stories of looking after their grandchildren. Engaging with the judiciary and traditional rulers to try and tackle the issue of harmful traditional practices. All those things that kept me grounded in the lived realities of the people, I left behind. I left behind my dreams of engaging in mainstream politics and being a vessel for change, bolstered after attending the Beijing World Conference on Women in 1995 in China, and being inspired by the thousands of women who went on to demand equal rights for women and girls.

Parents, siblings, friends and community, I left them all behind too. At the time, I don't think I consciously thought I was going to be away for a very long time. The journey was only meant to be for a few years for me and my husband to advance our academic education and explore different opportunities. It felt like the right thing to do at the time. So I took my skills, my experience and passion with me. I took my values with me. I took my heritage with me. And I left.

THERE WAS NO
BLACK IN THE
UNION JACK,
BUT THE TREES
KNEW MY NAME.

10

My crossing

I have experienced my own crossing. Like my grandparents and parents before me, I took to travelling. I have crossed rivers and oceans to arrive in this land that I now call home. I am not simply where I have been, but where I am and where I am going and so, even here, I must look to see what pieces I can pick up and make them part of my heritage.

When I first arrived in the UK to be here for a few years, I went through a period of disillusionment. It was in this country that I really became aware of my Blackness, not just as a colour, but as a social construct that was used to justify my treatment as a second-class citizen in a democratic society with democratic values and ideals. I had been aware of race, but had never experienced it as a heavy burden to carry.

I remember trying to get a job. By this point I had both my first and my second degrees, and had worked in Zambia on women's empowerment and economic development. As I had attended the University of Warwick in Coventry, and my husband was there, it was a natural destination for me to come back to. I was convinced that I could get a job. I went to a few employment agencies, but didn't get very far. One day, one of the recruitment consultants told me that I needed some UK-based experience. 'Anything, even cleaning experience, would be better than the experience that you currently have,' she said. To say that I was shocked, is an understatement. I could not quite believe what she was saying. I was at the beginning of picking up new pieces, but it was not going to be easy.

There were times when I thought I would be beaten up by a system that didn't want me. There were times when it felt it easier to accept the identity this system wanted me to have. One of weakness, poverty, nothingness; a second-class citizen. Yet each time I faltered, I would remember words, actions and stories from Sekuru, Mbuya and my mother. Stories that told me I was connected to a greater story. Stories that reminded me I was connected to humanity and nature: 'Remember Amanda,' Sekuru and then my own mother's voice would fill my mind: 'Wherever you go, the trees and the earth know your name. So, if you forget who you are, just remember what I have told you and you will be fine.' Powered by these pieces of my history, I found the strength to keep walking forward on my journey.

I eventually decided to train as a care worker to get the UK-based experience I was told I needed, and I worked in care homes, nursing homes and hospitals. I met many women like me from the continent of Africa, all highly educated but unable to get jobs in their fields of expertise, resorting to re-training and working as care assistants. As with everything, you can pick up some pieces to help you grow or you can close your eyes. This time of my life was deeply humbling. It took me into the heart of how people in my new home lived and thought. What their values were and the gaps between what they said and what they did. I was struck by how adult children could put their elderly parents in a home and leave them there without ever visiting them. It was painful to see, and in talking to those in the homes, you would hear the sadness in the elderly men and women residents. You would see the pictures of when they were young and full of life and dreams. I learned to see my work as a calling. There was much need for being human, but it wasn't all about learning, nor was it respectful.

At times I would find some who thought that being served by a Black African girl was their entitlement. They would make comments and refer to the good old days, how things used to be and how all was now lost. But I had to work and, for myself, I had to do my job well and with heart. I needed a job, I needed to put food on the table and I needed the work experience in the UK. Eventually, I also realized that I was in this position to learn something different and pick up some additional values that I would need as I was building me. These elderly people had worked hard to build their country. Some were stuck in a world of their own; they had found a place in their past where they were happy and free and went back into that place. I did my work with a smile on my face and with commitment, but please do not for a second consider this a justification for their views and their disrespect of my person. No. Not at all. This was simply my refusal to fight that particular battle; my instinct for survival, my desire to live and fight another day. Deep down, I knew God was not done with me yet. I was discovering what it meant to be not just a Black African woman, but one living in the UK.

I remember working a night shift and in the morning when close to the end of our shift, the permanent staff member who had worked the shift with me had to write some handover notes. 'How do you spell "and"?' she asked me. It sounds unbelievable, I know. The whole night we had worked very well together. She was very conscientious and worked judiciously to ensure that all the residents received the best treatment and service they needed. She was very human. In further conversations, it was clear she had not gone very far with academic education, but had excelled in the education of life. I learned some things of value from people I never thought I would. She didn't have much material wealth, but she had plenty of heart to share, yet still she looked at me and saw a Black woman who didn't belong. She was surprised that I had gone to school and stayed a little longer than she had. She was not sure where to place me – there was no Black in the Union Jack.

I would leave my shift early in the morning and, depending on where I had worked that night, I would walk to the station to wait for my bus home. Walking in the early hours, the trees would raise their ears to listen to my dejected step as I walked with my head down. I would hear the whispers as the leaves quietly moved in communication with each other, 'I thought that was Amanda, the daughter of Juliet?', one tree would say to others. 'That's what I thought too,' another would respond. 'No, it can't be her, she looks too defeated and lost. I thought Amanda was confident and vibrant. I thought she knew who she was and that we know her as well.'

The trees would go on, the lighter branches swaying with the slight winter breeze. 'Why don't you call her name and see if she is the one, maybe ask the wind to help you speak louder.' And swish, as the cold wind swept past, I would lift my head and look around. 'You see,' the trees would say, 'I told you she was the one'. I sometimes imagined that as the trees would communicate with each other here, they were also able to communicate with the trees in my grandfather's village. I imagined Sekuru out in the fields or sitting outside by the fire having his evening cup of tea. He would hear the trees talking about me and would know if things were going well and when they were not; I knew I needed to find breakthrough. As the branches moved from side to side and the leaves made loud whispers, I ran down the road as the bus arrived just in time. Getting on the bus, I would look back to the trees and smile. Yes, there was no Black in the Union Jack, but the trees knew my name.

SHE IS
THE WORLD.

11

The Black sisterhood

Aside remembering that the trees know my name, discovering Black sisters that share some of my experiences in the UK has been invaluable in making this country my home; we all need sisters to stand with in solidarity and role models to help pave the way.

'Who are your role models?' It's a question I get asked a lot. And, every time I am, I feel the sense of expectation that I will mention the popular names such as Mother Theresa, Eleanor Roosevelt, Maya Angelou, Harriet Tubman or Sojourner Truth. Of course, these women are extraordinary; they achieved a great deal and helped change the course of history. When I am asked that question, though, the very first people I think of are the women that I have seen and related to most of my life. Women like my mother, my Mbuya, my aunties. Women who have left a lasting impression on me, transferring their knowledge and values to me at the most formative times in my life. What I learned from them can never compare to any inspiration I get from people that I read of in literature; those characters simply complement or affirm the foundation upon which I stand. I want it to be acceptable to mention those closest to you as the people who have shaped and inspired you.

From my mother and Mbuya I took strength for granted. I saw entrepreneurship in action. My mother owned and ran a bus for public transport to pay school fees. She taught women how to grow oyster mushrooms in their spare rooms. She made and continues to make peanut butter and has a garden that is always flourishing. She inherited a strong sense of identity and personhood. My mother was widowed at a tender age of 24 years old. She refused to remarry any man who would not accept her children and their place in her life. My mother is a brave and courageous woman, no ordinary individual. She is the woman who gave birth to me, cared for me, struggled for me and continues to carry the cross of motherhood, which means that she will always worry about my wellbeing, irrespective of where I am, what I do or what I achieve. She, like other women who had a similar heritage whose stories will never be told, is a mosaic of stories, knowledge and leadership. As I talked to friends about this heritage, I saw a common and shared thread in values.

In speaking to a friend of mine in Zambia whose mother was Ndebele, he told me: 'I have always been proud of my heritage. Why? My mum represented everything a kid needs to grow up and be progressive. For instance, her values on hard work, initiative foresight and faith. The older I grow, especially beyond 50, the more I think of her contribution to my life. It's because of her, despite her low education, that I learnt my math, by selling food to people who worked in downtown Lusaka. From the caravan and her chicken sales our family home was acquired. From there her *kalembula* (a vegetable) sales ensured she never had to depend on anyone until her death. Her raw faith in God sustained her in the best and worst times.' As I spoke to other friends, I further discovered that many of my peers with Zimbabwean heritage seemed to share the same narrative and experience regarding the values of their parents. I think it is something we have taken for granted, something that needs to be recognized and appreciated. This was a generation who were uprooted, found themselves in a foreign land, and yet preserved what was good and wholesome of their own culture, and were able to pass it on and instil it in their progeny. They were extraordinary people.

On my journey of discovery, I have met other and different African women of all ages and they have given me a piece of themselves unreservedly, because that is what African women do. They share with you a bit of themselves so that you know they have walked a similar path and they have survived. While they may not all have been of the same value base as my mother and others of her kind, they were nevertheless the custodians and bearers of pieces of knowledge, ideals and values that were important in my evolution as a woman, as an African woman and as a Black African woman.

The Black African woman represents to me the struggles and the achievements, the vulnerabilities and the resilience, the injustices and the compassion, that is reflected in the contradictions of a world at war with itself. Wherever she has ended up in the world, the base experiences are similar. Much that is wrong and inhuman has been thrown her way and still she refuses to be defeated. To experience all these emotions in one lifetime and still be whole is to have incredible inner strength and wisdom. She is the world. It is therefore a privilege to be counted as one and to contribute to her stories.

I want to talk about these women, not only as individuals but as an ideal –an ideal that the world pretends does not exist, the world chooses to ignore. I have met women, young and old,

Black African women from the diaspora, from west Africa, from east Africa, from southern Africa, and they have played their part in affirming my personhood. They have played their role in showing me different outlooks where integrity means more than words, where sisterhood is a joyful and fulfilling sacrifice and where love is sacred.

I remember the year that Obama won the elections as the first Black president of the United States of America. I was in Coventry and on my way into town. While I stood at the bus stop waiting for the bus, another Black woman walked up and stood quietly behind me as if we were in a queue. For a few minutes we hesitated and kept on looking at each other. Then we both turned and hugged each other, laughed and screamed our joy. I didn't know this woman from Eve, but I knew her, and she knew me. There was an understanding there of a struggle so deep it has been passed on from generation to generation. It is a struggle that must be fought and conquered. On this momentous day, we had found another piece. Just writing about it makes me want to jump up and let the bubbles of joy come through again, as they did then. Importantly, we looked at each other and saw ourselves as two Black women who shared a heritage of struggle. And we had just overcome. We made it!

'It's such a shame there are so few African women of integrity in leadership,' I once heard a colleague say. You can imagine what went through my mind: What! My Goodness! What a thing to say without evidence! I was outraged. I could agree to the fact that there are not nearly enough African women in global positions of leadership, and that we do not hear much about the achievements of the many African women leading innovation, change and resilience in the different spaces. In fact, I recently attended the Sam Sharpe lecture, which is given once a year during Black History month. The focus was on Repression, Resistance and Reparation, and as the lecturer delivered the final parts of her talk she called out the names of the women who had given their lives in the fight against slavery. You would normally not hear of them, they are not named among the abolitionists. Instead, they are nameless, faceless and unknown. What I could not and cannot agree with is the statement that there are far fewer African women of integrity in leadership than there are in the general leadership population. The entire story of my heritage and identity is filled with Black African women of integrity. You find them all over the place. In schools, they are working with very little material, they strive to ensure that as many children as possible get the best education that can be provided. They are not just teachers, they are mothers, counsellors, comforters and they inspire. They are creative and innovative, having to teach with no teaching aids, they look around them and from nature they create ways of learning. In the communities, they lead. When the water is far, they find ways of organizing themselves to ensure that they can share and work together. Exasperated, frustrated and hurt, I resorted to expressing myself on my social media:

'The idea that there are African women out there, whose leadership values and practices are very much aligned, who walk the talk, appears to still be a 'phenomenon' that surprises – why is that? It offends me greatly ... that the default position appears to be a scarcity rather than an abundance ... let us bring out our stories of women's leadership that inspires and that is true even beyond the private space! Not only for ourselves but for the sake of our young ones, who see this inspiration in the home, only to have quashed in the 'real' world. When they look for us in the papers, in the media, in the public places, we are not as visible and yet we are there ... ordinary women doing extraordinary things ... transforming lives with determination and resilience ...'

I could give you chapter and verse of women in my life who have shown extraordinary leadership in their homes, their communities and elsewhere. They have done so with integrity and resilience in a world where the decks are stacked against them. For almost always little to no pay, no recognition, little consideration, lots of hassle, lots of belittlement, criticism and God knows what else, many of them plod along and try to ensure that they lead from the back for fear of being considered too strong and wanting to take control. They deliberately hide their light so that it does not shine above others (whether these others are men or women of other races).

To be an economically, emotionally and politically emancipated human being is not the comfortable narrative that the mainstream wants to hear of when they talk about African women. The mainstream is more comfortable with the false narrative that says African women are suffering, illiterate, cannot lead, poor, victims and a lot of other labels. Accepting the fact that there are many African women with brilliant leadership skills and experiences at different levels would mean questioning why many of them are not afforded the opportunities to be in the big decision-making spaces.

The injustice of it all, the inequalities that it produces and the stench that stifles innovation, growth and laughter, is what gets me. It gets me every time. It is the smell of oppression. That is what has led millions of women to try and navigate the different spaces, however great or small and by whatever means to get to the end alive! It is the horrible, disgusting and fatal smell of greed which causes us to see women as things or empty vessels to be used. It is what fundamentally stands between significant investment for gender equality and the pitiful rhetorical political statements made to appease voters while resources are recklessly used for self-serving agendas, agendas that perpetuate the exploitation of natural resources, the unfair and unequal distribution of resources and the unjust use of power. African women have been leading and are leading in exemplary fashion in different parts of the world and at different levels. It is when I look at such examples, however hidden and out of the public eye they may be, that I get a lot of energy that gives me strength and motivation to continue to do what I can do, to continue to look for spaces and opportunities where women can take on leadership and make it transformational.

When I relocated from Zambia to the UK, Gladys, a woman of substance and integrity whom I hold in very high regard, gave me a name and told me that should I ever find myself without a network of support, I should contact Akina Mama wa Afrika who were at the time based in London. For a couple of years, I forgot about the name and plodded along trying to get my act together and find space in the system to pursue my career and make a living. One of my *Aha!* moments came when I finally recalled the name and called their offices. For several weeks I kept calling and leaving messages. Lo and behold, a woman called me back and talked to me about a workshop that would bring together a number of women from Africa who were living in the UK, to focus on personal empowerment. So when the workshop came in February 2002, I went along to Birmingham and gained far more than I expected. I came away with a list of acquaintances I had spent a week with, and from there I was able to build a network of friends and sisters who would hold my hand at different stages of my personal and professional development. To this day, I shall be eternally grateful for that movement of sisters.

The workshop opened deeply buried memories. Memories of a strong identity and background that had gone into hiding when faced with multiple structural and institutional hammers whose job was to destroy the very essence of my self-esteem. They came out running from the depth of me, screaming and kicking to be let free to roam and explore, as they were meant to have been doing all along. Memories of my mother telling me how much I could achieve as she walked me to school in Lusaka. Memories of my Sekuru telling me how important it was that the trees knew my name. It was a glorious experience and feeling of freedom with emerging clarity of me, myself and I.

My step changed as I walked in Coventry with a newfound bounce. I was not too sure at that point where I was going, but hey, I knew that I was on my way to somewhere. I was moving forward, an African woman on a mission. I had picked up yet some more pieces from my past, my heritage and from my new home in the UK.

I KNOW THAT I
AM HERE FOR A
CHOSEN PURPOSE.

12

Held by faith

I was moving forward with my life in the UK and faith found me again. For me, it always does and each time I am reminded of Paul's letter to the Philippians where he says, 'Being confident of this very thing, that He who begun a good work in you will complete it …'[9] Having found a church community in Coventry, I had acquired a new family of friends. I just knew God was not done with me yet and that the different pieces that I had picked up along the way were converging into one. My understanding and conviction about justice, women's rights and equality could not be separated from my understanding of faith and the word of God. I became convinced, as I remain today, that God is the author of justice, respect, love and dignity.

I was appointed as leader of the Women's Ministry in Church and would use my position to flag up issues of gender-based violence. It was not always well received, but it was important to have a conversation. The Seventh Day Women's Ministry focused on strengthening the spiritual journey of women in the Church. It was therefore vital that we address the issues that were hindering that spiritual growth and well-being. While women can lead through preaching, teaching and holding different positions, there was a wall of silence on

---

9   Philippians 1:6.

violence against women. But we were able to rally the women in the church to create safe spaces to have dialogues on matters that affected them. I think during that period I realized that God does not abhor character and strength. He loves and gives strength. He calls us to reason together with him and to tell him the desires of our hearts. He is not a God that bullies, and therefore it was important for me to find my voice in the Church.

I refuse to be less than what God intended me to be. When you take the power and strength that comes from my heritage as a Black African Woman and place them in the heart of faith, I find that the values of my heritage are aligned with the values that my faith in God gives me. What I refuse is to be in fear of looking at the two as mutually reaffirming. We were indoctrinated into believing that everything that was traditional was bad and evil. This is a lie, one that we have lived with for far too long. One that, like the question, 'Where are you from?' is meant to rob you of your values and who you are – your identity. The actual question is a reference to the belief that nothing good can come out of Blackness.

In studying scripture, I saw how my parents' lives were a manifestation of the word of God; they lived a life of integrity, caring and truth. I wanted my life to reflect what God would have me do and be. As far as possible, I wanted to be true to the spirit and intent of the Bible message. Knowing that, as human beings, we are weak and make mistakes, but that through God we are made strong and we can therefore strive to be what He wants us to be. For me, I have concluded that that is the purpose of our existence: to live the life that God would have us live. To reflect the beauty of his creation, living in harmony with each other and with nature. Looking after what he gave us and following his instructions.

At times it has been difficult to talk about my faith so openly. In the UK at least, for a while it felt like there was a subtle but real dislike for anything that is faith. There have been and continue to be many grey areas when it comes to religion. In the case of Christianity, the faith and the church are held, in the court of public opinion, as one and the same thing.Yet there is a subtle but very fundamental difference. The Church as an institution has interpreted the Bible in so many ways and has been a beacon of hope for many people over many generations. It has stepped into the gap when there were no healthcare services or education. It has been there to broker peace and to help bring reconciliation among warring groups. It has brought hope to millions of people at a time when hope was all they could have.

Yet let us not be blind or behave as ostriches, lest we are seen as hypocrites and cowards. The Church has many times allowed itself to be an instrument of oppression and wrongdoing, and for too long. It has allowed itself to be corrupted – be it as the provider of the 'permission'[10] for enslavement during the transatlantic slave trade, as a vehicle for oppression during the colonial period, or indeed, as a way of continuing to create wealth and centralized power through capitalism. The Church has benefitted from the injustices experienced by millions of people worldwide, and particularly by Black people and those with darker skin. It has permitted its role as a custodian

---

10 For example the *Dum Diversas*, Papal Bull issued by Pope Nicholas V, authoris-ing the Portuguese to conquer the pagans in africa and consign them to perpetual servitude.

and protector of the most vulnerable to be corrupted and manipulated, becoming a marketplace where the word of God is traded. The Church, that place which should be a sanctuary, a place of hope, trust and safety, consciously or unconsciously has been complicit in doing harm. As the prophet Nathan said to David following his ill deeds with Bathsheba and the killing of Uriah,[11] 'Why did you despise the word of the Lord by doing what is evil in his eyes?' As the Church has started recognizing its role in this injustice, so too must it accept its role to lead changing the narrative and unjust practices. The Church must now struggle with that legacy and contend with the imperative to heal and restore. One could argue that justice demands that what has been taken must be restored *fourfold*.[12]

Faith, on the other hand, is what millions of people have on a day-to-day basis. It is their belief in the divine goodness that lies inherent in human beings. The goodness that, if it is well nurtured, will generate the coherence that we need in the world today. Faith, for me, is knowing that there is God and that he lives inside me. That He shapes and moulds those who believe in him to be the best versions of themselves. Faith goes beyond institutions – in fact, it exists in spite of institutions. There is a chasm that has formed between faith and religious institutions and it has formed over a long time. However, we are living in times when this divide must be bridged. Institutions need faith, it is the only way that restoration and justice will see the light of day. A faith that surpasses all understanding; a faith that is driven to do good, to love mercy and to walk justly

---

11 2 Samuel 11.

12 Luke 19:8.

with God.[13] Now more than ever, as millions of people, young and old, lock arms and say no to racial injustice, gender-based violence, the exploitation of people and natural resources, we must strive not just to do good but to be good. Now is the time.

The Church and other faith groups now have an opportunity to reclaim the good that faith stands for. They can help the world to experience a healing from the collective trauma that has been caused by centuries of manipulating the word of God, centuries of capitalism that puts power and wealth in the hands of the few at the expense of the multitude and our shared home. Silence and inaction are no longer an option.

In my journey, I have experienced silence. When wrongs are being perpetrated against me, colleagues sit around the same table and remain silent, that is difficult. When Black and ethnic minorities are disproportionately impacted on by disease and poverty, and those who are supposed to speak out against racial injustice remain silent, one wonders. Yes, I have experienced silence. And across that silence, God comes through. God hears and answers prayers. God never gives up on us, and I know it is important to not give up on him.

One of the greatest pieces for me on this journey of identity has been discovering and developing a relationship with Him. I am ever learning and being amazed at His grace and love. It has played such a central part in my life as it continuously brings the different pieces together. It is the thread that knits my fabric and weaves it into a beautiful pattern. His Grace is sufficient for me, His power is perfected in my weakness.[14]

---

13 Micah 6:8.

14 2 Corinthians 12:9.

Each day, each week, every month and every year, it gets better and better. Even when I slip up, faith finds me again and again. There have been times here that have been difficult and others where God has swung open doors for me to step through, such as securing my job at Christian Aid. Through everything the process has been a refining of my humanity; I know that I am here for a chosen purpose.

HUNDREDS OF
YEARS OF
MESSAGING,
HURT AND SOUL
EROSION HAVE
LEFT US WITH
A MAMMOTH
MOUNTAIN
TO CLIMB.

13

Unconscious brokenness

The UK is also a place I have chosen to call home, embracing it like an adopted child for all it is; the good, the bad, the ugly. Yet, like many others, I have spent much time feeling disillusioned by the reality of living here as an African in the diaspora. *Maybe the values that I had been told about while working in Zambia about the ideals of democracy, about values of inclusion were wrong? Maybe the truth I had learnt that every human being is equal and should be able to enjoy the exercise of the human rights, was one big lie?* Though these questions plagued me, I wonder perhaps, whether it was not so much a lie but a dream and aspiration that even the Western societies are still grappling with. I believe my pieces were solid and real. Instead what was shaken were my views of what this Western society stood for. Or at least who their institutions were and what they meant to do to me. Others like me, in this my new home, also looked at me as less than whole.

As I try to navigate different spaces professionally and personally, I come across behaviours that should not make sense, but I have learnt to take as the norm. We speak of unconscious biases and prejudices. When we look at others and judge them on the basis of the colour of their skin. We see this all over the world. Who cares if the lives of the people in the Amazon forests are threatened because of the fires – they are simply indigenous people of Black origin and thus their lives are graded less than important? Instead, we rush to rebuild Notre Dame, deeming it more important than the lives of these people and the world's largest biodiverse rainforests. The lives of the Black community in the US are easily expendable and Black children in the UK can wallow in the deprivations that dog their lives, or remain in care because they are not desired enough to be adopted. As a Black African woman leading a British charity whose mission is to reach out to those suffering from extreme poverty and experiencing immeasurable injustice, I cannot disconnect myself from the pain of what is happening. This is not just about the US; it is about racial injustice everywhere. Beyond the injustices that are the immediate focus of the organization I work for. I must use my voice to call out institutional failures to address racial oppression.

The realities of racial discrimination are deeper than ever before, except that we have become better at creating a façade that reflects what we think it should really look like. The Truth and Reconciliation Commission (TRC) in South Africa was applauded as a great initiative that heralded the birth of a rainbow nation. The reality tells a different story. While it provided a platform and space for the nation and its individuals to begin the process of healing, talk about the wrongs of the apartheid regime and find forgiveness and reconciliation, the process fell short of being the catalyst and springboard for dismantling systemic and institutionalized marginalization of Black South Africans. Several decades down the line and the systemic and structural divisions remain unresolved. The social and economic realities tell stories of a broken people living with open wounds and struggling to find a way through, their frustrations expressed in violence against each other, against women, against children and against anybody who might be seen as different, weaker and therefore an easy target. The search for justice, equality and dignity remains elusive for many Black South Africans.

There are so many examples picked up from all over the world, but when another Black woman looks at me and believes that because they are an African American or because they are Black British from the Caribbean, they are therefore of more value than me, a Black African woman, then it makes me pause. When an Asian woman looks at me and breathes a sigh of relief than she is not as Black as me or that she is not African otherwise it would be hell to pay, it makes me stop. And when another African Black woman looks at me and sees me as of less worth because they are slightly lighter in complexion than I am, I just want to cry. Crying for the depth of unconscious brokenness of a people. Hundreds of years of messaging, hurt and soul erosion have left us with a mammoth mountain to climb to remove the rubbish, untruths and rebuild replacing them with wholesome values and truths.

Global economic systems and models have evolved. From slavery to colonialism to capitalism. Or have they? Is it just another manifestation of the same concept? The continued exploitation of millions by a few? With the human being at the centre as a product to be graded, sold and purchased. Your grading determines what your life is worth, what rights you can enjoy, what services you must receive, what rules must be respected and how much your dignity is worth. Not all products are equal – that is the fundamental and perhaps the biggest lie that has been told to enable slavery, colonialism and capitalism to flourish. For me as a woman of faith, it goes against everything that I believe in – that every human being is created equal and with innate worth. When over 80 per cent of people in the world identify themselves with one faith or another, on what premise have we allowed a dominant narrative by a few, a narrative that places these few above the law of life, to be our modus operandi?

We have allowed this system that created the brokenness in the first place, to continue to deepen the wounds, pretend to bring solutions while all the time profiting from the collective trauma that comes from this unconscious brokenness. Unconscious because for many of us, this is all we have ever known. This is what we have learnt in our homes, in schools and on the streets of life. It is reinforced by institutions. When a BBC presenter can openly treat a Black politician 'differently', and despite a level of public outrage, refuse to apologize and get away with it. It speaks volumes. It is perhaps time we call it what it is – causing hurt, damage, destroying people – and it is not unconscious, it is systemic.

On all fronts, heritage, values, economy, politics, social tolerance, it's all on a path going nowhere. With our total disregard for the planet we have pressed the self-destruct button. And those who are dying first are those who contributed the least to this crisis. Greed and arrogance are the true cause – a deadly combination that cannot fathom the idea that there are other better and more humane ways of existing on this earth that we all call home. Ways and knowledge to be learned from those who are downtrodden and those with apparently little knowledge, because they have not been able to write it in the parameters that have been set out by a few.

Many of us, including those who are as indigenous as can be to this new home, can see now that where their ancestors once appeared to be bold and brave as they searched for more knowledge of the world around them, it is now clear that this search was driven by greed and an obsession to conquer and exploit everything that came within their reach, including people and land. Their braveness was in fact greed and arrogance, based on a belief that they had all the good knowledge and that their way was the only way. Assumptions that humility and not aspiring to have more and more was a weakness. Describing nations of people as primitive and backward because they lived a life of temperance and chose to live in harmony with nature. Because they did not walk around clothed in regalia that costs lots of money and did not eat food that was processed.

This arrogance and greed has led to the deaths of millions of people, the loss of balance between people and planet and one that continues to this day to find new ways of robbing people of their dignity and the planet of its ability to sustain life. Where we once thought of them as wealthy, we now know that all they had was money and no real wealth of humanity. Yet like every human group across the world, you always find a light shining on a hill to help find a humane pathway for people to walk on.

Yes, there are stories of hope and defiance. There are those who remember and those who have read of values and ideals and together they dream of how to overcome these untruths that seek to still a heritage of good things. In my travels I have met such people. Women who are defying the odds by staying alive and finding ways of living. I have spoken to young people who have dreams about a future. And I too, want to be part of a future. One that speaks of healing, community, sustainability, mutual respect and diversity. We must change. It will take a long time, but each one of us knows what is right. We are created equal and with innate worth. We also have innate goodness and knowledge of what is right. We must dig deep and bring out that which is right and wholesome and true. That is what will develop solutions that are sustainable. It will heal the planet and it will heal the people. It is idealistic, but nothing short of that will save the world from a path that it has currently set itself.

IN THE HEART OF THE KARANGA HOMESTEAD, I WAS RAISED.

I was taught to speak and laugh with grace. To fight with spirit and to love with passion. The Karangas were determined that they would make their imprint and they did. The Ngonis were absent, or so people thought. But look closely, yes, much closer, and you will see that they were there. Everything that they stand for was imprinted. Imprinted on to their daughter by a determined mother. She taught her daughter about the Ngonis. She taught her about the clan of the eagle. The eagle that has presence, is distinct, powerful, bold and soars high. She shaped and moulded her into a daughter of the Ngonis. A daughter of my ancestors, I am a Ngoni woman. Nachisale is my name.

14

So where are we really from?

'So where are we really from?' It's a simple question but there are no simple answers. It may be a question you've never been asked before. Like me, it may be a question you've been asked countless times. Yet if you look hard enough, you'll see that we are all trying to answer it.

Everywhere, every day, people are trying to find that one story that makes them them. But as they look at one piece, they don't see the many other pieces that are their gemstones of history, values and knowledge. Whatever that one thing is that defines them or another, they see only the one, dictating a one-track story that should no longer hold anybody captive. Rather, the uncertainties of many pieces should cause us to rejoice that every day is different, and when we gain new knowledge, we can then achieve the best version of ourselves that the world needs.

Everyone has many parts that form the puzzle that is a person or a community. Some parts we remember, others are so painful that we don't want to talk about or even remember them. We bury them so deep that they are only visible in the totality of who we become rather than in the words we use. For some, you look at your ancestors and find them wanting. You have experienced the wasteful practices of your people. You struggle to find new meaning and new ways to co-exist with others in peaceful and mutually respectful ways. You are taking steps to change the direction of travel. Someone once said, *you must learn to struggle and then struggle to learn.* The world around me now must struggle to learn what humane looks and feels like and then learn to struggle to make what is humane the new normal.

It is easy to see that everyone is grappling to understand their identity; it's human. For a long time, I have listened to different elements of my story being told to me by my mother and grandparents. I have also heard snippets from others who have perhaps walked a similar journey. I have felt the inner struggle of finding myself and my identity. Now I know that this journey has been about allowing that identity to emerge from within me and take root in a world of mixed narratives of who is acceptable and who is not, giving myself permission to celebrate the different determinants of this identity without guilt, shame or arrogance.

I truly believe my story didn't start in a country, it started in the mind of God where he shaped me and spoke me into being. As a woman of faith, I believe that he created every part of me, wonderfully and beautifully, to be a manifestation of his love. As for where I've been and where I'm going, I see now that there is no end, just pieces to be picked up.

Like you, I must surely unearth my heritage as it lives within me. I must understand it, take what is good for me and the future, nurture it and live it. I must celebrate it and all along, I must share it. The pieces are not broken. To the contrary, they are meant to be pieces, different and beautiful, some with sharp edges, others rounded and others in varying shapes yet to be named. I have so many different and beautiful pieces that make up who I have become. They were built around the fire with stories of love, integrity and community. They were consolidated with care and nurturing, like a fire that burns slowly within me. A kaleidoscope of music and songs, colours and shapes – my identity is fanned by continuous sources of energy from different lands, lessons and experiences. Like you, I am not just one thing and one thing only. I am many things. I am a living being and the pieces that will eventually complete everything that I am meant to be are not yet all made. Some are still in the making and some others are only in the mind of God who is yet to speak them into existence.

My stories of stories are about courage, about the vulnerability to learn new things and new ways of life. They are about living with people and among people, learning to forgive an injustice so great it transcends generations and continues to hurt. They are about all of this and more, and they are not just for me. They are for my children and their children. The world they live in, and the world to come, has many broken pieces. If they look only for the whole, then they will lose out. There are stories all around us, from all walks of life.

'But where are you really from?' I hope that in reading these pieces you have been able to judge me based on 'the content of my character' rather than 'the colour of my skin' and the continent of my 'origin'. I pray this book has encouraged you to pick up your own pieces, that it has helped you see that we have far more that unites us than could ever divide us. For those Black African women who read this, I hope it reaffirms you. For women in general who read this, I hope that you can see yourself in this Black African woman. And for the rest, I hope that you are inspired to ask the question: 'Who are you?' rather than 'Where are you really from?'

WE HAVE A VISION OF A WORLD IN WHICH EVERYONE IS TRANSFORMED BY CHRISTIAN KNOWLEDGE

As well as being an award-winning publisher, SPCK is the oldest Anglican mission agency in the world.

Our mission is to lead the way in creating books and resources that help everyone to make sense of faith.

Will you partner with us to put good books into the hands of prisoners, great assemblies in front of schoolchildren and reach out to people who have not yet been touched by the Christian faith?

To donate, please visit www.spckpublishing.co.uk/donate or call our friendly fundraising team on 020 7592 3900.

An easy way to get to know the Bible

'For those who've been putting aside two years in later life to read the Bible from cover to cover, the good news is: the most important bits are here.' Jeremy Vine, BBC Radio 2

The Bible is full of dramatic stories that have made it the world's bestselling book. But whoever has time to read it all from cover to cover? Now here's a way of getting to know the Bible without having to read every chapter and verse.

No summary, no paraphrase, no commentary: just the Bible's own story in the Bible's own words.

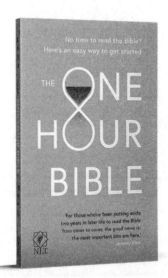

'What an amazing concept! This compelling, concise, slimmed-down Scripture is a must for anyone who finds those sixty-six books a tad daunting.'
Paul Kerensa, comedian and script writer

'A great introduction to the main stories in the Bible and it helps you to see how they fit together. It would be great to give as a gift.'
Five-star review on Amazon

The One Hour Bible
978 0 281 07964 3 • £4.99

 spck.org.uk   /SPCKPublishing   @SPCKPublishing   @SPCK_Publishing